Biology

Teaching Resources
Unit 9

PEARSON

Prentice
Hall

Upper Saddle River, New Jersey
Boston, Massachusetts

ISBN 0-13-203404-2

1 2 3 4 5 6 7 8 9 10   10 09 08 07 06

To the Teacher

The Teaching Resources unit booklets have been designed to help you teach *Prentice Hall Biology*. Each unit book consists of materials that have been designed to stimulate students' interest in biology, develop their critical thinking, and teach them basic science skills. The unit books will accommodate a wide range of student abilities and interests.

Each teaching resource unit book contains the following:

- Lesson Plans (for each section)
- Reading and Study Workbook A (includes section summaries, section worksheets, and a chapter vocabulary review written at grade level)
- Adapted Reading and Study Workbook B worksheets (Includes section summaries, key concept worksheets, and a chapter vocabulary review written at a sixth-grade reading level)
- Section Review Worksheets
- Enrichment Worksheets
- Graphic Organizers
- Chapter Tests (Includes two tests for each chapter—Test A for students performing on or above grade level; Test B for students performing on or below grade level)
- Unit Tests (two tests for each unit—Test A and Test B)
- Answer Key (for section review worksheets, enrichment worksheets, graphic organizers, and chapter tests.)
- Graphic Organizer Transparencies (generic reproducible masters)
- Transparency Planner (Full-color preview of all the transparencies that support the unit)

Unit 9 Chordates
Chapter 30 Nonvertebrate Chordates, Fishes, and Amphibians

Chapter 31 Reptiles and Birds

Chapter 32 Mammals

Chapter 33 Comparing Chordates

Chapter 34 Animal Behavior

LESSON PLAN 30–1 (pages 767–770)

The Chordates

Section Objectives

- **30.1.1 Identify** the characteristics that all chordates share.
- **30.1.2 Explain** what vertebrates are.
- **30.1.3 Describe** the two groups of nonvertebrate chordates.

Vocabulary chordate • notochord • pharyngeal pouch • vertebra

Local Standards

---

1 FOCUS

Vocabulary Preview
Explain the origin of the word *notochord*. Also explain the meaning of *pharyngeal*.

Targeted Resources
- ❏ Transparencies: **452** Section 30–1 Interest Grabber
- ❏ Transparencies: **453** Section 30–1 Outline

---

2 INSTRUCT

Build Science Skills: Applying Concepts
Students identify chordate structures in pictures of various chordate embryos. **L2**

Build Science Skills: Observing
Students locate and examine the vertebral column in various skeletons. **L1 L2**

Make Connections: Physics
Describe how muscles and bones work like levers to produce movement. **L2 L3**

Use Visuals: Figure 30–3
Students identify chordate structures in the diagrams of tunicates in Figure 30–3. **L1 L2**

Build Science Skills: Classifying
Students diagram a lancelet and explain why it is a nonvertebrate. **L1 L2**

Targeted Resources
- ❏ Reading and Study Workbook: Section 30–1
- ❏ Adapted Reading and Study Workbook: Section 30–1
- ❏ Teaching Resources: Section Summaries 30–1, Worksheets 30–1
- ❏ Transparencies: **454** Chordate Cladogram, **455** Figure 30–1 The Generalized Structure of a Chordate
- ❏ **NSTA** *sci*LINKS Nonvertebrate chordates

---

3 ASSESS

Evaluate Understanding
Orally quiz students to name the chordate characteristics and describe the nonvertebrate chordates.

Reteach
Students use the chordate diagram in Figure 30–1 to reinforce their understanding of the Vocabulary words.

Targeted Resources
- ❏ Teaching Resources: Section Review 30–1
- ❏ *iText* Section 30–1

LESSON PLAN 30–2 (pages 771–781)

Fishes

Section Objectives

- **30.2.1 Identify** the basic characteristics of fishes.
- **30.2.2 Summarize** the evolution of fishes.
- **30.2.3 Explain** how fishes are adapted for life in water.
- **30.2.4 Describe** the three main groups of fishes.

Vocabulary cartilage • atrium • ventricle • cerebrum • cerebellum • medulla oblongata • lateral line system • swim bladder • oviparous • ovoviviparous • viviparous

Local Standards

1 FOCUS

Reading Strategy
As students read, have them note Vocabulary words and meanings and sketch some of the diagrams.

Targeted Resources
❏ Transparencies: **456** Section 30–2 Interest Grabber
❏ Transparencies: **457** Section 30–2 Outline

2 INSTRUCT

Build Science Skills: Using Models
Students create a model of a fish. **L1 L2**

Use Visuals: Figure 30–7
Students make inferences about the adaptations of the fishes illustrated in Figure 30–7. **L2**

Make Connections: Physics
Students experiment to determine the body shape that best moves through water. **L2 L3**

Make Connections: Chemistry
By reviewing osmosis, students better understand the importance of the kidneys in regulating water in the body of fishes. **L1 L2**

Demonstration
Students observe a model of a swim bladder. **L2**

Build Science Skills: Classifying
Students devise their own classification system for a sample of different fishes. **L2**

Targeted Resources
❏ Reading and Study Workbook: Section 30–2
❏ Adapted Reading and Study Workbook: Section 30–2
❏ Transparencies: **458** Circulation in a Fish, **459** Figure 30–11 The Internal Anatomy of a Fish
❏ Teaching Resources: Section Summaries 30–2, Worksheets 30–2, Enrichment
❏ **NSTA** *sci*LINKS Fishes

3 ASSESS

Evaluate Understanding
Students write a sentence about the characteristics of fishes. They also make a table about the groups of fishes.

Reteach
Students create a concept map about ways in which fishes are adapted to live in water.

Targeted Resources
❏ Teaching Resources: Section Review 30–2
❏ *i*Text Section 30–2

LESSON PLAN 30–3 (pages 782–789)

Amphibians

Section Objectives
- **30.3.1 Describe** what an amphibian is.
- **30.3.2 Summarize** events in the evolution of amphibians.
- **30.3.3 Explain** how amphibians are adapted for life on land.
- **30.3.4 Describe** essential life functions in amphibians.
- **30.3.5 Name** the main groups of living amphibians.

Vocabulary cloaca • nictitating membrane • tympanic membrane

Local Standards

1 FOCUS

Vocabulary Preview
Give students the origins of the words *nictitating* and *tympanic*. Then, have them infer the locations of these two membranes.

Targeted Resources
- ❑ Transparencies: **460** Section 30–3 Interest Grabber
- ❑ Transparencies: **461** Section 30–3 Outline
- ❑ Transparencies: **462** Concept Map

2 INSTRUCT

Use Visuals: Figure 30–23
Use Figure 30–23 to reinforce the adaptations amphibians have for living on land. **L2**

Build Science Skills: Comparing and Contrasting
Students create a graphic organizer to show differences in the form and function of fishes and amphibians. **L1** **L2**

Demonstration
Students observe the internal anatomy of a frog. **L2**

Make Connections: Physics
Demonstrate how changes in air pressure force air into a frog's lungs. **L2** **L3**

Build Science Skills: Comparing and Contrasting
Students contrast characteristics of the three amphibian groups. **L1** **L2**

Targeted Resources
- ❑ Reading and Study Workbook: Section 30–3
- ❑ Adapted Reading and Study Workbook: Section 30–3
- ❑ Teaching Resources: Section Summaries 30–3, Worksheets 30–3
- ❑ Transparencies: **463** Figure 30–26 The Life Cycle of a Frog
- ❑ Lab Worksheets: Chapter 30 Exploration
- ❑ Lab Manual A: Chapter 30 Lab
- ❑ Lab Manual B: Chapter 30 Lab
- ❑ **PHSchool.com** Chordates and vertebrates

3 ASSESS

Evaluate Understanding
Students answer questions about amphibian characteristics and adaptations.

Reteach
Students label a frog diagram with adaptations for life on land.

Targeted Resources
- ❑ Teaching Resources: Section Review 30–3, Chapter Vocabulary Review, Graphic Organizer, Chapter 30 Tests Levels A and B
- ❑ **iText** Section 30–3, Chapter 30 Assessment
- ❑ **PHSchool.com** Online Chapter 30 Test

Chapter 30 Nonvertebrate Chordates, Fishes, and Amphibians

Summary

30–1 The Chordates

A chordate is an animal with four features for at least some stage of its life:

- A **hollow nerve cord** runs along the back of the body. Nerves branch from it and connect to organs and muscles.
- A **notochord** is a support rod that runs just below the nerve cord.
- **Pharyngeal pouches** are paired structures in the throat. In some chordates, they become gills.
- A **tail** that extends beyond the anus is the fourth common feature.

Most chordates are vertebrates. **Vertebrates** have a backbone made up of vertebrae. The backbone replaces the notochord and supports and protects the spinal cord. It also gives muscles a place to attach. **Two groups of chordates do not have backbones.**

- **Tunicates** are ocean-living filter feeders. Adult tunicates have no notochord or tail. Larval tunicates have all chordate characteristics.
- **Lancelets** are small, fishlike animals. Adult lancelets have all four chordate characteristics. They also have a definite head region.

30–2 Fishes

Fishes are aquatic vertebrates; most fishes have paired fins, scales, and gills. Jaws and paired fins were important developments in fish evolution. Jaws improved defense and expanded food choices. Paired fins improved control of body movement.

Adaptations to aquatic life include various modes of feeding, specialized structures for gas exchange, and paired fins for locomotion.

- Feeding. Fishes feed in many ways. They may be herbivores, carnivores, parasites, filter feeders, or detritus feeders. One fish may feed in several ways, depending on the food available.
- Respiration. Most fishes breathe with gills. Gills have many tiny blood vessels that provide a large surface area for gas exchange. Fishes pull water in through the mouth. The water then moves over the gills and out of the body through openings in the sides of the pharynx.
- Circulation. Fishes have a closed circulatory system. It pumps blood in a loop from heart to gills to the body and back to the heart. The heart consists of two chambers: an atrium and a ventricle.

- Excretion. Most fishes get rid of wastes as ammonia. Some wastes diffuse through the gills into the water. Others are removed from the blood by kidneys. Kidneys also help fishes control the amount of water in their bodies.
- Response. Fishes have well-developed nervous systems. The brain has several parts. Unlike other chordates, in fish the **cerebrum** is primarily involved in smell. The **cerebellum** coordinates body movements. The **medulla oblongata** controls the functioning of many internal organs. Most fishes also have a **lateral line system** that senses currents and vibrations in the water.
- Movement. Most fishes move by contracting muscles on either side of the backbone. Fins push the fish forward and help it steer. Many fishes have a gas-filled organ called a **swim bladder** that keeps them from sinking.
- Reproduction. Fishes reproduce in several ways. Eggs may be fertilized externally or internally, depending on the species.
  - **Oviparous** fishes lay eggs. The eggs develop and hatch outside the mother's body.
  - In **ovoviviparous** fishes, the fertilized eggs develop inside the female. The embryos are fed by yolk in the egg. The young are then "born alive" from the mother's body.
  - In **viviparous** fishes, embryos develop inside the mother. They get food from the mother's body, not from an egg. They are also born alive.

There are three classes of fishes.
- Lampreys and hagfishes are **jawless fishes.** Their bodies are supported by a notochord. They do not have true teeth or jaws. They are parasites and scavengers.
- The **cartilaginous fishes** include sharks, rays, and skates. These fishes have a skeleton made of cartilage. Most also have toothlike scales covering their skin.
- **Bony fishes** have skeletons made of bone. Most bony fishes are ray-finned fishes. Their fins have thin, bony spines that are joined by a thin layer of skin.

30–3 Amphibians

An amphibian is a vertebrate that, with some exceptions, lives in water as a larva and on land as an adult. Amphibians breathe with lungs as adults, have moist skin that contains mucous glands, and lack scales and claws.

Early amphibians evolved several adaptations that helped them live at least part of their lives out of water. Bones in the limbs and limb girdles of amphibians became stronger, permitting more efficient movement. Lungs and breathing tubes enabled amphibians to breathe air. The sternum, or breastbone, formed a bony shield to support and protect internal organs, especially the lungs.

Other amphibian characteristics include:
- Feeding. Amphibian larvae are filter feeders or herbivores. They have long, coiled intestines that help them break down plant matter. Adults are carnivores and have a much shorter intestine.
- Respiration. In most larvae, gas exchange occurs through the skin as well as gills. Lungs usually replace gills as an amphibian becomes an adult. In adults, some gas exchange occurs through the skin and the lining of the mouth.
- Circulation. Amphibian hearts have three chambers: a left atrium, a right atrium, and a ventricle. The circulatory system of adult amphibians forms a double loop. The first loop carries oxygen-poor blood from the heart to the lungs and returns oxygen-rich blood to the heart. The second loop carries oxygen-rich blood from the heart to the body and returns oxygen-poor blood to the heart.
- Excretion. Kidneys remove wastes from blood. Urine passes through tubes called ureters into the cloaca. From there, it either passes directly to the outside or is stored in a small urinary bladder.
- Reproduction. Amphibian eggs lack shells. In most amphibians, the female usually lays eggs in water, where the male fertilizes them. The eggs hatch into larvae, often called tadpoles. Tadpoles change into adults.
- Nervous system. Amphibians have well-developed nervous systems and sense organs. Frogs have very good vision. Tympanic membranes, or eardrums, receive sound vibrations.

There are three amphibian groups: salamanders, frogs and toads, and caecilians.
- Salamanders have long bodies, four legs, and long tails.
- Frogs and toads do not have tails and can jump. Frogs live close to water, whereas toads often live in moist wooded areas.
- Caecilians do not have legs. Caecilians live in water or burrow in moist soil.

Chordate Structure

At some stage in their lives, all chordates have four characteristics: a hollow nerve cord, a notochord, pharyngeal pouches, and a tail that extends beyond the anus. The nerve cord runs along the animal's back. The notochord is a supporting rod. Most chordates have a notochord only as embryos. Pharyngeal pouches are paired structures in the throat region.

Color the notochord *yellow. Color the* hollow nerve cord *blue. Color the* pharyngeal pouches *red.*

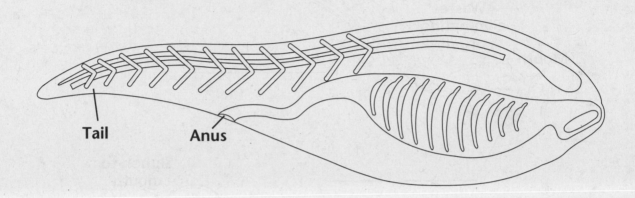

Tail   **Anus**

Use the diagram to answer the questions.

1. From which structure do nerves branch off? Circle the correct answer.

   nerve cord   pharyngeal pouches

2. In some chordates, slits connect the pharyngeal pouches to the outside of the body. In aquatic chordates, what may these slits develop into to use for gas exchange?

   _____

3. For what purpose do many aquatic chordates use their tails?

   _____

Nonvertebrate Chordates

Tunicates are one of the two groups of chordates that do not have backbones. Larval tunicates have all four characteristics of chordates, although they lose many of them as adults.

Label the hollow nerve cord, notochord, pharynx with gill slits, *and* tail *on the diagrams. Remember that not all of the structures will appear in both diagrams.*

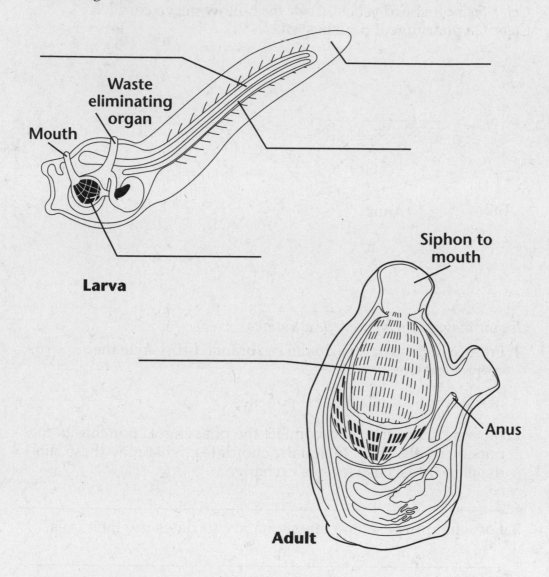

Larva

Adult

Use the diagrams to answer the question. Circle the correct answer.

1. Which structure common to chordates appears in both the larval and adult tunicates?

   notochord   pharynx with gill slits

Common Fish Structures

Although there are many kinds of fish, most of them have three features in common: paired fins, scales, and gills. The gills may be covered by an operculum, or gill cover. The diagram below shows one type of fish, called an African cichlid.

Label five fins, *the* scales, *and the* operculum *in the diagram.*

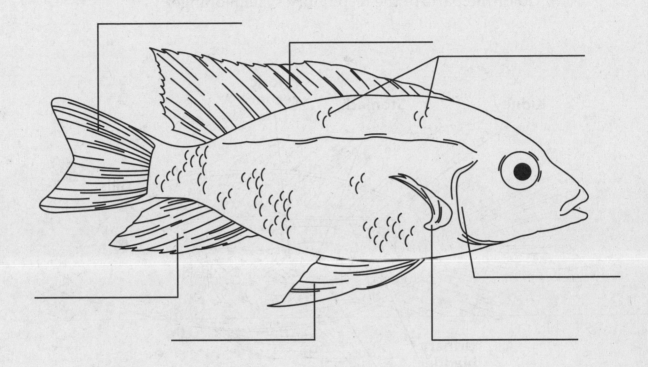

Use the diagram to answer the questions.

1. Which structures are used for movement? Circle the correct answer.

   fins   gills

2. Which structures are used for gas exchange? Circle the correct answer.

   gills   scales

3. What is the role of gills?

   _____

   _____

Form and Function in Fishes

Fish have specialized body systems for digestion, excretion, and respiration.

Look at the labeled structures on the fish diagram below. Color these structures according to the prompts below.
- Color the parts of the digestive system blue.
- Color the parts of the excretory system yellow.
- Color the parts of the respiratory system orange.

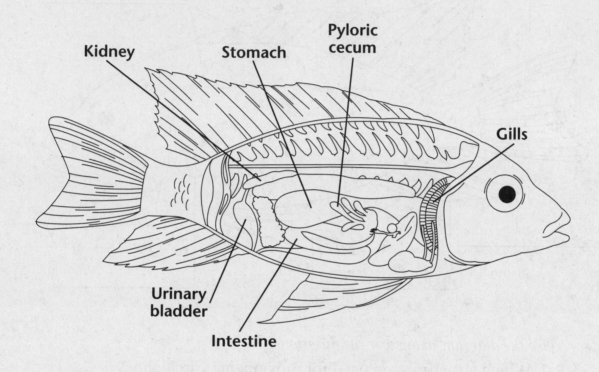

Use the diagram to answer the questions. Circle the correct answer.

1. Which structure is part of the digestive system?

   gills   pyloric cecum

2. Which structure is part of the excretory system?

   stomach   urinary bladder

3. What is one function of the kidney?

   filter wastes from blood   gas exchange

Amphibian Land Adaptations

As amphibians evolved from lobe-finned fishes, they developed adaptations that helped them spend parts of their lives out of water. These included adaptations to their lungs, bones, and skin.

Use the words below to identify how each adaptation helps amphibians survive on land. The first one has been done for you.

> more efficient movement
> permits gas exchange
> protects internal organs

Body Part	Adaptation	How It Helps Survival
lungs	blood vessels, folds that increase surface area, breathing tubes	allows amphibians to breathe air
limb bones	stronger limb and pelvic bones	
chest bones	development of sternum, or breastbone	
skin	thin, richly supplied with blood vessels; watery mucus secreted by glands	

Answer the question. Circle the correct answer.

1. For how long does an amphibian live on land?

its entire life   part of its life

Frog Digestive System

Adult frogs are mostly carnivorous. Their digestive systems are specialized to digest other organisms.

Use the words below to label the structures in the frog's digestive system.

large intestine	pancreas	stomach
liver	small intestine	

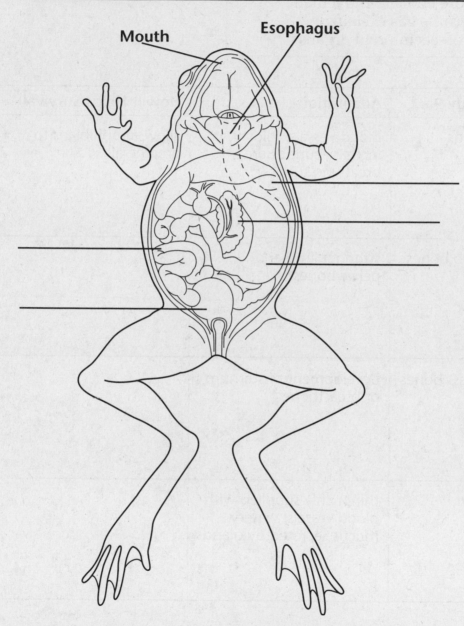

Mouth   **Esophagus**

Use the diagram to answer the question. Circle the correct answer.

1. Which is the first organ food passes through after it leaves the esophagus?

pancreas   stomach

Fish and Amphibian Circulation

Complete the table to compare fish and adult amphibian circulatory systems. The first one has been done for you.

	Fish	**Adult Amphibian**
Structure of system	single loop	double loop
Organs that bring oxygen to blood	gills	
Number of atria in heart	one	
Do oxygen-poor and oxygen-rich blood mix in the heart?		yes

Answer the questions.

1. How many ventricles do the hearts of amphibians and fishes

   have? _____

2. Which describes the blood that passes through a fish's heart? Circle the correct answer.

   oxygen-rich   oxygen-poor

Frog Life Cycle

Like most other amphibians, frogs spend part of their life cycle living in water and part living on land. Frogs use gills for respiration when they live in the water, and lungs when they live on land.

Color the stages of the frog's life cycle that are lived on land brown. Color the stages that are lived in the water blue.

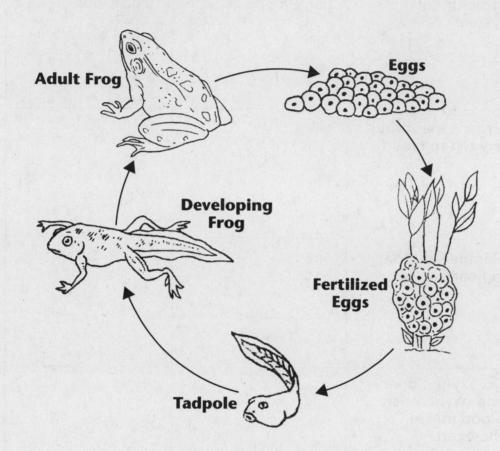

Use the diagram to answer the questions. Circle the correct answer.

1. Where do frog eggs hatch into tadpoles?

in the water   on land

2. Which respiratory organs do adult frogs use?

gills   lungs

Chapter 30   Nonvertebrate Chordates, Fishes, and Amphibians

Vocabulary Review

Matching   *In the space provided, write the letter of the definition that best matches each term.*

_____ **1.** cartilage

_____ **2.** cerebellum

_____ **3.** notochord

_____ **4.** ovoviviparous

_____ **5.** vertebra

a. a segment of the backbone

b. part of the brain that coordinates body movements

c. fishes whose eggs develop inside the mother's body and whose young are born alive

d. long, supporting rod that runs through the body just below the neve cord

e. strong tissue that supports the body and is more flexible than bone

Completion   *Use the words below to fill in the blanks with terms from the chapter.*

atrium	chordates	tympanic membrane
cerebrum	cloaca	viviparous

6. Fishes, amphibians, reptiles, birds, and mammals are all

_____.

7. A large muscular chamber of the heart called a(an)

_____ serves as a one-way compartment.

8. Voluntary activities of the body are controlled by the

_____, a portion of the brain.

9. In _____ animals, the embryos stay in the mother's body after fertilization and obtain the nutrients they need from the mother's body.

10. The large muscular cavity at the end of an amphibian's large

intestine is the _____.

11. Another name for eardrum is_____.

Summary

30–1 The Chordates

A chordate is an animal that has, for at least some stage of its life, a hollow nerve cord, a notochord, pharyngeal pouches, and a tail.

The hollow nerve cord runs along the back of the body. Nerves branch from it and connect to organs and muscles.

The notochord is a long supporting rod that runs just below the nerve cord. Most chordates have a notochord only as embryos.

Pharyngeal pouches are paired structures in the throat. In some chordates, they develop into gills.

Most chordates are vertebrates. Vertebrates have a backbone made of segments called vertebrae. The backbone replaces the notochord. The backbone gives support and protects the spinal cord. It also gives the muscles a place to attach.

Two groups of chordates do not have backbones. Tunicates are filter feeders that live in the ocean. Adult tunicates have neither a notochord nor a tail. Larval tunicates have the chordate characteristics.

The other group of chordates without a backbone is the lancelet. Lancelets are small, fishlike animals. Adult lancelets have all four chordate characteristics. They also have a definite head region.

30–2 Fishes

Fishes are animals with backbones that live in water. They usually have paired fins, scales, and gills.

Fishes were the first vertebrates to evolve. The evolution of jaws and paired fins was the most important development in fish evolution. Jaws improved defense and expanded food choices. Paired fins gave more control of body movement.

Fishes have various modes of feeding. Fishes are herbivores, carnivores, parasites, filter feeders, and detritus feeders. One fish may even have several different modes of feeding, depending on the food available.

Most fishes breathe with gills. Gills have many tiny blood vessels. This provides a large surface area for oxygen and carbon to be exchanged. Most fishes breathe by pulling water through the mouth and pumping it over the gills and out through openings in the sides of the pharynx.

Fishes have a closed circulatory system that pumps blood in a single loop—from the heart to the gills, from the gills to the body, and back to the heart. The heart is made up of four parts: the sinus venosus, atrium, ventricle, and bulbus arteriosus. The ventricle is the actual pumping portion of the heart. The atrium is a one-way compartment for blood that is going to enter the ventricle.

Most fishes get rid of wastes as ammonia. Some wastes pass through the gills into the water. Other wastes are removed from the blood by the kidneys. Kidneys also help fishes control the amount of water in their bodies.

Fishes have well-developed nervous systems. The brain has several parts. The olfactory bulbs and cerebrum are involved with the sense of smell. The optic lobes process information from the eyes. The cerebellum coordinates body movements. Most fishes have a lateral line system that senses currents and vibrations in the water.

Most fishes move by contracting muscles on either side of the backbone. Fins propel the fish forward and help it steer. Many fishes have a gas-filled swim bladder that keeps them from sinking.

Fishes reproduce in a number of ways. Their eggs are fertilized either externally or internally, depending on the species. Some lay eggs. They are called oviparous. In ovo-viviparous fishes, the eggs develop inside the female. The embryos are fed by an attached yolk sac. In viviparous fishes, the embryos get their food from the mother's body, not from an egg.

All fishes can be classified into three groups: jawless fishes, cartilaginous fishes, and bony fishes. Lampreys and hagfishes are jawless fishes. Their bodies are supported by a notochord. They do not have true teeth or jaws. They are parasites and scavengers.

The cartilaginous fishes include sharks, rays, and skates. All members of this group of fishes have a skeleton made of cartilage. Most also have toothlike scales covering their skin.

Bony fishes have skeletons made of bone. Almost all bony fishes belong to the group known as the ray-finned fishes. Their fins have thin, bony spines that are joined together by a thin layer of skin.

30–3 Amphibians

Amphibians have some—but not all—of the adaptations necessary to live on land. As larvae, they live in water. As adults, they live on land. Adult amphibians breathe with lungs and have moist skin that has mucous glands. They do not have scales and claws.

Early amphibians had several adaptations that helped them live on land. Leg bones became stronger to hold weight and allow movement. Lungs and moist skin allowed them to get oxygen from air. The breastbone supported and protected internal organs.

Amphibian larvae are filter feeders or herbivores. They have long, coiled intestines. This helps them break down plant material. Adults have a much shorter intestine because they are carnivores.

In most larvae, gas exchange occurs through the skin as well as lungs. Lungs usually replace gills when an amphibian becomes an adult. However, some gas exchange occurs through the skin and the lining of the mouth.

In adult amphibians, the circulatory system forms a double loop. The first loop carries oxygen-poor blood from the heart to the lungs. It returns oxygen-rich blood to the heart from the lungs. The second loop carries oxygen-rich blood from the heart to the body and returns to the heart with oxygen-poor blood. The amphibian heart has three separate chambers: left atrium, right atrium, and ventricle.

Kidneys remove wastes from blood. Urine passes to the cloaca. From there, it either passes directly to the outside or is stored in a small bladder.

Amphibian eggs do not have shells. The female usually lays eggs in water. The male fertilizes them externally. The eggs hatch into larvae, which are often called tadpoles. Tadpoles gradually change into adults that live on land.

Amphibians have well-developed nervous systems and sense organs. Frogs have keen vision to spot and respond to moving insects. Tympanic membranes, or eardrums, receive sound vibrations.

The amphibian groups are salamanders, frogs and toads, and caecilians. Salamanders have long bodies, legs, and tails. Frogs and toads do not have tails and can jump. Caecilians do not have legs.

Chapter 30   Nonvertebrate Chordates, Fishes, and Amphibians

Section 30–1 The Chordates (pages 767–770)

Key Concepts
- What characteristics do all chordates share?
- What are the two groups of nonvertebrate chordates?

What Is a Chordate? (page 767)

1. List the four key characteristics of a chordate.

a. _____

b. _____

c. _____

d. _____

Use the diagram below to match the description of the chordate characteristic with its structure.

Structure

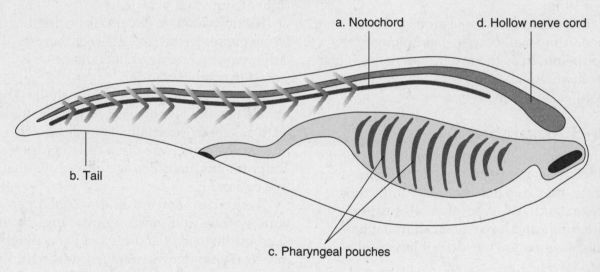

a. Notochord   d. Hollow nerve cord

b. Tail

c. Pharyngeal pouches

Description

_____ 2. Connects nerves to internal organs, muscles, and sense organs

_____ 3. Long supporting rod located just below the nerve cord

_____ 4. Paired structures in the throat region

_____ 5. Contains bone and muscle

Most Chordates Are Vertebrates (page 768)

6. What structure do most vertebrates have? _____

7. What chordate structure becomes the spinal cord in vertebrates? _____

8. The backbone is made of individual segments called _____ that enclose and protect the spinal cord.

9. Circle the letter of each sentence that is true about vertebrates.

   a. A vertebrate's backbone is part of an endoskeleton.

   b. The endoskeleton supports and protects the animal's body.

   c. The endoskeleton must be shed as the animal grows.

   d. The endoskeleton is made entirely of nonliving material.

Nonvertebrate Chordates (pages 769–770)

10. How are tunicates and lancelets similar to each other? _____
_____

11. What evidence indicates that vertebrates and nonvertebrate chordates evolved from a common ancestor? _____
_____
_____

12. Circle the letter of each characteristic found only in tunicate larvae and not in tunicate adults.

   a. tunic   c. hollow nerve cord

   b. tail   d. notochord

13. Is the following sentence true or false? Both larval and adult tunicates are filter feeders.
_____

14. Circle the letter of each characteristic found in lancelets.

   a. definite head region   c. notochord

   b. jaws   d. fins

15. Is the following sentence true or false? Lancelets use the pharynx for feeding and gas exchange. _____

16. How is blood moved through the body of a lancelet? _____
_____
_____

Reading Skill Practice

A Venn diagram is a useful tool to compare and contrast two things. Construct a Venn diagram to compare and contrast the characteristics of tunicates and lancelets. See Appendix A in your textbook, for more information about Venn diagrams. Do your work on a separate sheet of paper.

Section 30–2 Fishes (pages 771–781)

Key Concepts
- What are the basic characteristics of fishes?
- What were the important developments during the evolution of fishes?
- How are fishes adapted for life in water?
- What are the three main groups of fishes?

What Is a Fish? (page 771)

1. Write the function of each characteristic of fishes.

   a. Paired fins _____

   b. Scales _____

   c. Gills _____

2. Is the following sentence true or false? The characteristics of living fishes are very uniform and almost no diversity exists among fishes. _____

Evolution of Fishes (pages 772–773)

3. Circle the letter of each sentence that is true about the evolution of fishes.

   a. Fishes were the first vertebrates to evolve.

   b. Fishes arose directly from tunicates and lancelets.

   c. Fishes changed little during the course of their evolution.

   d. Early fishes were jawless and covered with bony plates.

4. Which period is known as the Age of Fishes?

   a. Cambrian   c. Silurian

   b. Ordovician   d. Devonian

5. Jawless fishes with little armor of the Devonian Period were the ancestors of modern _____ and _____.

6. Why were jaws an extremely useful adaptation? _____
_____
_____

7. A strong tissue that supports the body and is more flexible than bone is

   _____

8. Is the following sentence true or false? Paired fins gave fishes less control over their movement. _____

Form and Function in Fishes (pages 774–778)

9. What are the different modes of feeding found in fishes? _____
_____

10. Is the following sentence true or false? A single fish may exhibit only one mode of feeding. _____

Match the internal organ with its function.

Internal Organ	**Function**
_____ **11.** Pyloric ceca	**a.** Short tube connecting the fish's mouth to the stomach
_____ **12.** Intestine	**b.** Where food is first partially broken down
_____ **13.** Pancreas	**c.** Fingerlike pouches in which food is processed and nutrients absorbed
_____ **14.** Esophagus	**d.** Adds digestive enzymes and other substances to food as it moves through the gut
_____ **15.** Anus	**e.** Completes the process of digestion and nutrient absorption
_____ **16.** Stomach	**f.** Opening through which undigested material is eliminated

17. What does the capillary network in each gill filament provide? _____
_____
_____

18. Describe how fishes with gills exchange gases. _____
_____
_____
_____

19. The protective bony cover over the gill slit from which water is pumped out of a fish's body is called a(an) _____.

20. How do lungfishes survive in oxygen-poor water? _____
_____
_____

21. Is the following sentence true or false? Fishes have an open circulatory system.
_____

Match each chamber of the heart in fishes with its function.

Heart Chamber	**Function**
_____ **22.** Ventricle	**a.** Collects oxygen-poor blood from the veins
_____ **23.** Sinus venosus	**b.** Large muscular cavity that serves as a one-way compartment for blood entering the ventricle
_____ **24.** Bulbus arteriosus	**c.** Thick-walled, muscular chamber that is the actual pumping portion of the heart
_____ **25.** Atrium	**d.** Large, muscular tube that connects to the ventricle and moves blood through the aorta toward the gills

26. What form of nitrogenous waste do most fishes excrete?

_____

27. How does the function of kidneys in saltwater fishes differ from their function in

freshwater fishes? _____

_____

_____

Match the structures of the fish's brain with their functions.

Structure	Function
_____ **28.** Olfactory bulb	**a.** Controls the functioning of many internal organs
_____ **29.** Cerebrum	**b.** Primarily processes the sense of smell in fishes
_____ **30.** Optic lobe	**c.** Coordinates body movements
_____ **31.** Cerebellum	**d.** Involved with the sense of smell, or olfaction
_____ **32.** Medulla oblongata	**e.** Processes information from the eyes

33. Circle the letter of each sentence that is true about the sense organs of fishes.

a. Fishes have poorly developed sense organs.

b. Many fishes have chemoreceptors that sense tastes and smells.

c. Fishes have a lateral line system used for sensing sounds.

d. Some fishes can sense low levels of electric current.

34. What are two ways that fins help fish to move?

a. _____

b. _____

35. The streamlined body shapes of most fishes help reduce the amount of

_____ as they move through the water.

36. What is the function of the swim bladder? _____

_____

_____

37. In which mode of fish reproduction do the embryos develop inside the mother's body using the egg yolk for nourishment?

a. oviparous

c. viviparous

b. ovoviviparous

d. herbivorous

Groups of Fishes (pages 778–780)

38. Fishes are divided into groups according to _____ structure.

39. Complete the table about the groups of fishes.

GROUPS OF FISHES

Type	Description	Examples
	No true teeth; skeletons made of fibers and cartilage; keep their notochord as adults	
Cartilaginous fishes		Sharks, rays, skates
		Ray-finned fishes, such as flounder, angelfish, and flying fish and lobe-finned fishes, such as lungfishes and the coelacanth

40. Is the following sentence true or false? Hagfishes are filter feeders as larvae and parasites as adults. _____

41. Circle the letter of each characteristic of a shark.

   a. torpedo-shaped body

   b. secretes slime

   c. many teeth

   d. winglike fins

42. Is the following sentence true or false? Lobe-finned fishes have fleshy fins supported by bones that are sometimes jointed. _____

Ecology of Fishes (page 781)

43. Fishes that spend most of their lives in the ocean but migrate to fresh water to breed are called _____.

44. Fishes that live in fresh water but migrate to the ocean to breed are called

   _____.

Section 30-3 Amphibians (pages 782-789)

🔑 Key Concepts

- What is an amphibian?
- How are amphibians adapted for life on land?
- What are the main groups of living amphibians?

What Is an Amphibian? (page 782)

1. Is the following sentence true or false? Amphibian adults are fishlike aquatic animals that respire using gills. _____

2. Circle the letter of each characteristic of amphibians.

   a. scales   **b.** claws   **c.** moist skin   **d.** mucous glands

Evolution of Amphibians (pages 782-783)

3. List three challenges that had to be overcome by vertebrates colonizing land habitats.

   a. _____

   b. _____

   c. _____

4. List three adaptations that evolved in amphibians that helped them live at least part of their lives out of water.

   a. _____

   b. _____

   c. _____

5. Amphibians became the dominant form of animal life during the _____ Period, also known as the Age of Amphibians.

6. Why did most amphibian groups become extinct by the end of the Permian Period?

   _____

   _____

   _____

7. What three orders of amphibians survive today?

   a. _____

   b. _____

   c. _____

Form and Function in Amphibians (pages 784-787)

8. Circle the letter of each characteristic of a tadpole.

   a. carnivore

   b. herbivore

   c. long intestines

   d. short intestines

9. Circle the letter of each characteristic of an adult amphibian.

    a. carnivore   **c.** sticky tongue

    b. herbivore   **d.** long intestines

10. Briefly describe the path of food in a frog's digestive system.

_____

_____

_____

11. Circle the letter of each sentence that is true about respiration.

    a. In tadpoles, gas exchange occurs only through the skin.

    b. Lungs replace gills when an amphibian becomes an adult.

    c. Gas exchange in adults can also occur through the skin.

    d. All adult amphibians have lungs.

12. Amphibians have _____ that filter wastes from the blood.

13. Complete the captions in the diagram about the stages in the life cycle of a frog.

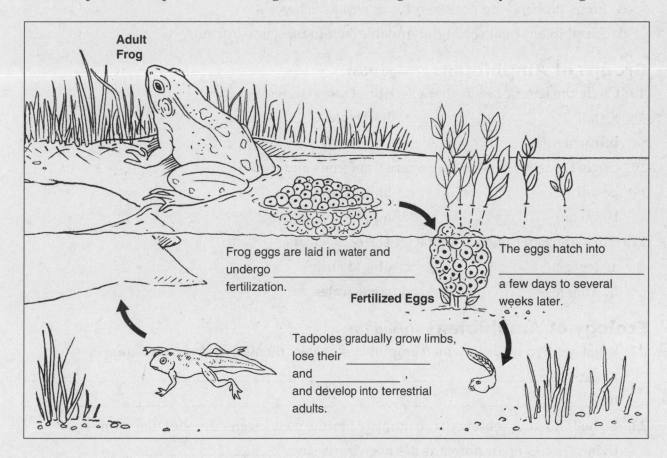

Adult Frog

Frog eggs are laid in water and undergo _____ fertilization.

Fertilized Eggs

The eggs hatch into _____ a few days to several weeks later.

Tadpoles gradually grow limbs, lose their _____ and _____ , and develop into terrestrial adults.

14. How is the first loop in the circulatory system of an adult amphibian different from the second loop? _____

_____

_____

Match the type of amphibian with its method of movement.

Amphibian	Method of Movement
_____ **15.** Tadpoles	**a.** Flattened tail for propulsion
_____ **16.** Adult salamanders	**b.** Well-developed hind limbs for jumping
_____ **17.** Frogs and toads	**c.** Legs push backward against the ground

18. Circle the letter of each sentence that is true about response in amphibians.

a. An amphibian's brain is structured very differently from a fish's.

b. An amphibian's eye is protected from damage and kept moist by the nictitating membrane.

c. Frogs probably do not see color as well as fishes.

d. Amphibians hear through tympanic membranes, or eardrums.

Groups of Amphibians (page 788)

19. Circle the letter of each characteristic of salamanders.

a. tail   **c.** herbivore

b. carnivore   **d.** short body

20. Circle the letter of each characteristic of frogs and toads.

a. tail   **c.** able to jump

b. no tail   **d.** adults have gills

21. Circle the letter of each characteristic of caecilians.

a. legless   **c.** able to jump

b. long legs   **d.** some scales

Ecology of Amphibians (page 789)

22. What are two ways in which amphibians protect themselves from predators?

a. _____

b. _____

23. Is the following sentence true or false? For the past several decades, the number of living species of amphibians has been increasing. _____

Chapter 30   Nonvertebrate Chordates, Fishes, and Amphibians

Vocabulary Review

Labeling Diagrams   *Use the following words to label the structures of the animal below:* nerve cord, notochord, pharyngeal pouches, *and* tail. *Then, complete the sentence.*

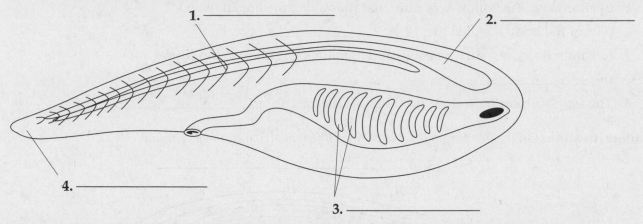

1._____

2._____

4._____

3._____

5. The animal diagrammed above is an example of a(an) _____.

Matching   *In the space provided, write the letter of the definition that best matches each term.*

_____ **6.** vertebrae

_____ **7.** cartilage

_____ **8.** atrium

_____ **9.** ventricle

_____ **10.** cerebrum

_____ **11.** cerebellum

_____ **12.** medulla oblongata

_____ **13.** lateral line system

_____ **14.** swim bladder

_____ **15.** oviparous

a. part of the brain responsible for voluntary activities

b. part of the brain that controls many internal organs

c. chamber of the heart into which blood enters from the body

d. method of development in which eggs hatch outside the mother's body

e. receptors in fishes that sense motion and vibrations in water

f. tissue that is softer and more flexible than bone

g. individual segments that make up the backbone

h. part of the brain that coordinates body movements

i. the actual pumping portion of the heart

j. gas-filled organ in fishes that adjusts buoyancy

Completion   *Fill in the blanks with terms from Chapter 30.*

16. In _____ animals, the eggs develop inside the mother's body, and the embryo uses the yolk for nourishment.

17. In _____ animals, the embryos develop inside the mother's body and obtain their nourishment from their mother, not the egg.

18. The muscular cavity at the end of the large intestine in amphibians is called the

_____.

19. Transparent eyelids, called _____ membranes, protect an amphibian's eyes underwater and keep them moist in air.

20. Amphibians hear through _____ membranes, or eardrums.

Chapter 30 Nonvertebrate Chordates, Fishes, and Amphibians   **Section Review 30-1**

Reviewing Key Concepts

Completion *On the lines provided, complete the following sentences.*

1. In chordates, the hollow structure that runs along the dorsal (back) part of the body is called the _____.

2. In some chordates, such as fishes and amphibians, gills develop from the _____.

3. The long supporting rod in chordates is called a(an) _____.

Identification *On the lines provided, identify the different structures of a chordate.*

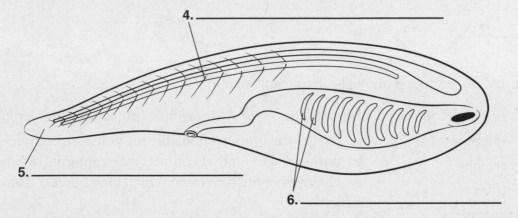

4. _____

5. _____

6. _____

Short Answer *On the lines provided, answer the following questions.*

7. How do lancelets and tunicates differ from most chordates?

_____

_____

8. Describe the differences between lancelets and tunicates.

_____

_____

Reviewing Key Skills

9. **Applying Concepts** What chordate characteristic is not displayed in most adult chordates?

_____

_____

10. **Inferring** Suppose you followed the development of an organism through its life cycle. What information would help you determine that it can be classified as a chordate?

_____

_____

Chapter 30 Nonvertebrate Chordates, Fishes, and Amphibians   Section Review 30-2

Reviewing Key Concepts

Completion *On the lines provided, complete the following sentences.*

1. Fishes are characterized by _____, which are

   used for movement, _____, which are used for

   gas exchange, and _____, which are used for protection.

2. Two important developments in the rise of early fishes were the

   evolution of jaws and _____.

3. In their modes of feeding, fishes are classified as _____,

   _____, parasites, filter feeders, and detritus feeders.

4. Several types of fishes have specialized organs that function as

   _____ to help them breathe out of water.

Identification *On the lines provided, identify each fish as* jawless, cartilaginous, *or* bony.

5. _____ shark

6. _____ lamprey

7. _____ lungfish

Reviewing Key Skills

8. **Comparing and Contrasting** How are ovoviviparous and viviparous methods of reproduction in fishes similar? How are they different?

   _____

   _____

   _____

   _____

9. **Comparing and Contrasting** How are anadromous and catadromous fishes similar? How are they different?

   _____

   _____

   _____

   _____

10. **Applying Concepts** What actions can jawed fishes perform that jawless fishes are unable to do?

   _____

   _____

   _____

Chapter 30 Nonvertebrate Chordates, Fishes, and Amphibians   **Section Review 30-3**

Reviewing Key Concepts

Completion *On the lines provided, write the word or words from inside the parentheses that best complete the sentence.*

1. As larvae, most amphibians live _____ (in water/on land).

2. Most adult amphibians breathe with _____ (gills/lungs).

3. Amphibians have _____ (moist/dry) skin.

4. Most amphibians _____ (have/lack) scales and claws.

Short Answer *On the lines provided, answer the question.*

5. Describe the adaptations that enabled amphibians to live part of their lives on land.

_____

_____

_____

Identification *On the lines provided, identify which group of amphibians—caecilians, salamanders, or frogs and toads—best completes the sentence.*

6. With fishlike scales in their skin, _____ are legless animals that feed on termites.

7. The amphibians known for their jumping ability are _____.

8. Classified as carnivores, _____ have long bodies and tails.

Reviewing Key Skills

9. **Applying Concepts** Describe how the three-chambered amphibian heart supplies the body with oxygen.

_____

_____

10. **Applying Concepts** Use your knowledge of amphibian respiration and reproduction to explain how the disappearance of many swampy areas at the end of the Permian Period caused many amphibian species to die out.

_____

_____

_____

**Chapter 30 Nonvertebrate Chordates, Fishes,   Chapter Vocabulary Review
and Amphibians**

Labeling Diagrams *On the lines provided in the diagram, label the cerebrum, the cerebellum, and the medulla oblongata.*

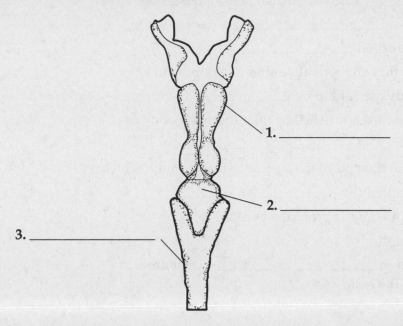

1._____

2._____

3._____

Completion *On the lines provided, write the word that best completes each sentence.*

4. An animal that has a hollow nerve chord, a notochord, pharyngeal pouches, and a tail that extends beyond the anus is classified as a(an)

   _____.

5. Most chordates have a(an) _____ only when they are embryos.

6. The paired structures found in the throat region of a chordate are the

   _____.

7. The strong tissue that supports the body, but is softer and more

   flexible than bone, is _____.

8. In vertebrates, the spinal cord is enclosed and protected by individual

   _____.

9. In the heart of most chordates, blood enters a chamber called the

   _____.

10. The thick-walled, muscular chamber that is the actual pumping

    portion of the heart is the _____.

11. The portion of the brain that coordinates body movement is the

    _____.

12. In most vertebrates, the part of the brain called the

_____ controls voluntary activities.

13. The sensitive receptor in most fishes that detects gentle currents and

vibrations in the water is called the _____.

14. In many bony fishes, the gas-filled organ that helps adjust their

buoyancy is called the _____.

15. Fishes that lay eggs are called _____.

16. Fishes that bear young that are born alive after developing in eggs

inside the mother's body are said to be _____.

17. Fishes in which embryos are nourished by their mother's body as

they develop are called _____.

18. In a frog, the structure at the end of the large intestine through which

wastes are expelled is called the _____.

19. The surface of the eye of a frog is protected by a(an)

_____.

20. Amphibians hear through _____ that are
located on each side of the head.

Chapter 30 Nonvertebrate Chordates, Fishes, and Amphibians   Enrichment

Shark Diversity

Of the approximately 30,000 species of fishes, over 350 are sharks. When you think of a shark, you may be reminded of the vicious fish portrayed in movies and on television. However, no more than 30 species of sharks are harmful to humans.

The species of sharks known to attack people most frequently are the great white shark, the tiger shark, the hammerhead, the bull shark, and the oceanic whitetip shark. The largest sharks—the whale shark and the basking shark—are not dangerous to humans. Although extremely large, they have very tiny teeth and feed on plankton and small fishes. Many other sharks are bottom feeders and eat crustaceans or other small prey.

The different species of sharks are identified by a variety of characteristics. For example, sizes are extremely diverse. The whale shark is approximately 15 m long. The smallest shark, *Squaliolus laticaudas,* is only about 15 cm long when fully grown.

Sharks are very successful predators because they can use a variety of senses to detect prey. Although their eyes are poorly adapted to seeing subtle movement in dim light, sharks compensate for this by having an acute sense of smell. The snouts of sharks are equipped with sensory organs that provide them with the ability to sense low-frequency vibrations, such as the movement of fishes in the water. Sharks can also detect weak electrical stimuli of the kind produced by most fishes. Many sharks can swim quite fast for short bursts of time. The blue shark has been observed swimming at over 64 km per hour. Such speeds enable many sharks to outswim their prey.

Some sharks gather in schools to feed. They may even migrate in schools. The schools are often divided by sex or age. Huge numbers of spiny dogfish sharks migrate each year from the Caribbean to the sub-Arctic. Other sharks, such as the tiger and great white, spend most of their time alone.

Scientists are still studying the role of sharks in the ocean ecosystem. Sharks are the garbage collectors of the ocean, because they often feed on wounded or dying fishes. However, sharks are also active hunters and consume healthy fishes as well. Many of the larger predators are known to attack and eat seals near the coastlines of warmer waters. Sharks are a diverse group and are currently in danger of being overhunted by humans. There is still much to learn about this fascinating group of fishes.

Evaluation *Answer the following questions on a separate sheet of paper.*

1. Some people think that all sharks pose a serious threat to humans and that sharks should be killed whenever they are encountered. Do you agree? Explain your answer.

2. What adaptations do sharks have that allow them to be successful in their environment? Explain your answer.

Chapter 30 Nonvertebrate Chordates, Fishes, and Amphibians   **Graphic Organizer**

Concept Map

Using information from the chapter, complete the concept map below. If there is not enough room for your answers in the concept map, write them on a separate sheet of paper.

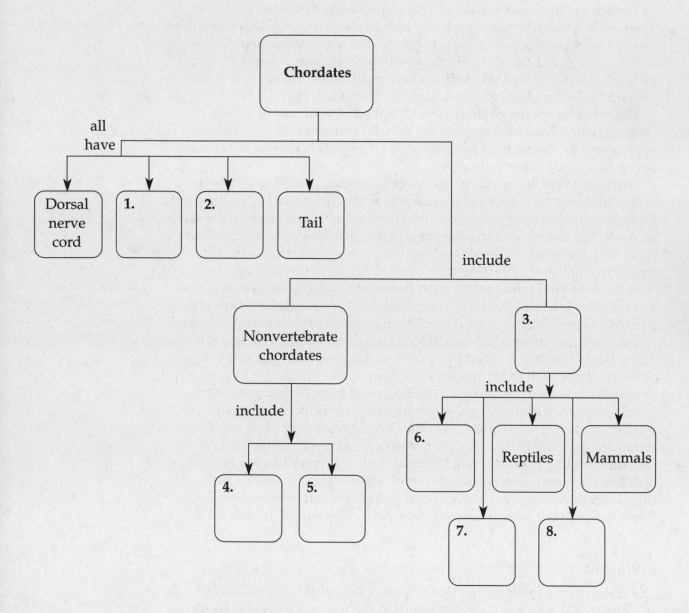

Chapter 30 Nonvertebrate Chordates, Fishes, and Amphibians **Chapter Test A**

Multiple Choice

Write the letter that best answers the question or completes the statement on the line provided.

_____ 1. Which of these chordate characteristics exists as paired structures?
  a. tail   c. pharyngeal pouch
  b. notochord   d. nerve cord

_____ 2. Which of the following statements about a vertebrate's skeleton is INCORRECT?
  a. It supports and protects the body.
  b. It is an endoskeleton.
  c. It grows as the animal grows.
  d. It is made entirely of nonliving material.

_____ 3. Lancelets belong to the phylum
  a. Urochordata.   c. Vertebrata.
  b. Cephalochordata.   d. Chordata.

_____ 4. In most fishes, the structures that are most important for obtaining oxygen from water are the
  a. scales.   c. lungs.
  b. gills.   d. vertebrae.

_____ 5. Fishes that lived during the late Cambrian Period
  a. lacked paired fins.
  b. had powerful jaws.
  c. had limbs.
  d. had soft bodies with little or no armor.

_____ 6. After passing through the gills of a fish, blood circulates through the rest of the body and then collects in the
  a. atrium.   c. bulbus arteriosus.
  b. ventricle.   d. sinus venosus.

_____ 7. Most fishes get rid of nitrogenous wastes by
  a. taking in ammonia through the gills and eliminating it from the kidneys.
  b. taking in water through the kidneys and eliminating ammonia from the gills.
  c. eliminating ammonia from the gills and from the kidneys.
  d. eliminating urine from the gills and ammonia from the kidneys.

____ **8.** Sharks, rays, and skates are alike in the
  a. foods that they eat.
  b. size and form of their teeth.
  c. shape of their bodies.
  d. composition of their skeletons.

____ **9.** Which feature distinguishes most fishes from most amphibians?
  a. a vertebral column
  b. scales
  c. breathing with gills during at least part of the life cycle
  d. living in water during at least part of the life cycle

____ **10.** The dominance of amphibians during the Carboniferous Period ended because
  a. many of their habitats disappeared due to climate changes.
  b. swampy fern forests became more widespread.
  c. amphibians were never very numerous during that period.
  d. amphibians did not evolve from the first forms that climbed onto land.

____ **11.** Which of the following is NOT an adaptation of early amphibians?
  a. strong bones in the limbs
  b. strong bones in the pelvic girdle
  c. a bony cage around the internal organs
  d. gills

____ **12.** Which of the following structures are missing from caecilians?
  a. lungs   c. legs
  b. kidneys   d. eyes

____ **13.** Which of the following is NOT a characteristic of an amphibian's circulatory system?
  a. two loops
  b. heart with three chambers
  c. right atrium and left atrium
  d. complete separation of oxygen-rich and oxygen-poor blood

____ **14.** A frog's tympanic membranes would be most useful for
  a. enabling the frog to jump long distances.
  b. filtering wastes from the frog's blood.
  c. listening to the mating calls of other frogs.
  d. keeping the frog's eyes from drying out on land.

Name______________________________ Class_________________ Date ____________

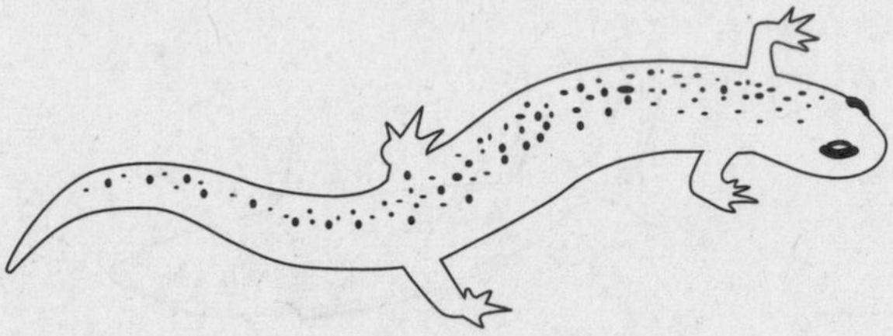

Figure 1

____15. Amphibians like the one in Figure 1 are
a. herbivores as larvae and carnivores as adults.
b. carnivores as larvae and herbivores as adults.
c. herbivores as larvae and adults.
d. carnivores as larvae and adults.

Completion

Complete each statement on the line provided.

16. In fishes and amphibians, gills develop from slits that form in the ________________.

17. One basic characteristic of fishes is the presence of ________________, which they use to obtain oxygen from water.

18. If a vertebrate is aquatic as a larva and terrestrial as an adult, it is a(an) ________________.

19. One adaptation of amphibians for life on land is the presence of mucous glands in the skin, which can help protect amphibians from ________________.

20. In a frog's heart, blood from the body enters the ________________.

Short Answer

In complete sentences, write the answers to the questions on the lines provided.

21. In vertebrates, how does the front end of the spinal cord differ from the rear end?

____

____

____

22. Identify one feature of early fishes from the Cambrian Period that was probably useful as a defense against predators.

____

____

____

23. Describe the structure and list two functions of the pyloric ceca of fishes.

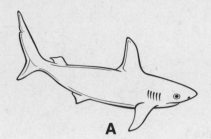

A

_____

_____

_____

_____

24. Distinguish between anadromous and catadromous fishes.

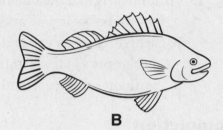

B

_____

_____

_____

_____

_____

25. Describe the composition of the skeleton of each fish in Figure 2.

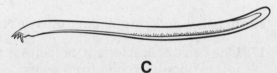

C

_____

Figure 2

_____

_____

_____

_____

Using Science Skills

Use the diagram below to answer the following questions on the lines provided.

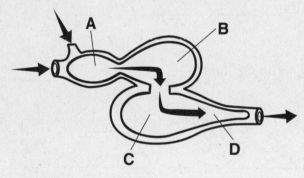

Figure 3

26. **Interpreting Graphics** Identify the heart chambers labeled A through D in Figure 3.

_____

_____

_____

27. **Applying Concepts** In Figure 3, is the blood that enters the chamber labeled A rich in oxygen or poor in oxygen?

_____

28. **Interpreting Graphics** In Figure 3, which chamber is the actual pumping portion of the heart?

_____

_____

29. **Applying Concepts** To what vessel does the chamber labeled D connect? (This vessel is not shown in Figure 3.)

_____

_____

30. **Applying Concepts** In Figure 3, what are the first organs that blood passes through after passing through the chamber labeled D?

_____

_____

Essay

Write the answer to each question in the space provided.

31. Contrast the structure of an adult lancelet and an adult tunicate.

32. Explain how having jaws was a useful adaptation for early fishes.

33. Name the five main parts of a fish's brain, and describe the function of each part.

34. How are worldwide amphibian populations changing today? What possible explanations have been proposed to explain the change?

35. Describe the circulation of blood through the body of an adult amphibian. Include the chambers of the heart in your description.

Chapter 30 Nonvertebrate Chordates, Fishes, and Amphibians   **Chapter Test B**

Multiple Choice

Write the letter that best answers the question or completes the statement on the line provided.

_____ 1. In chordates, the long supporting rod that runs through the body is called the
    a. nerve cord.
    b. notochord.
    c. pharyngeal pouch.

_____ 2. A vertebrate is any chordate that has a
    a. backbone.
    b. notochord.
    c. hollow nerve cord.

_____ 3. The two groups of nonvertebrate chordates are
    a. tunicates and lancelets.
    b. skates and rays.
    c. frogs and toads.

_____ 4. Most fishes are characterized by each of the following EXCEPT
    a. a cartilaginous skeleton.
    b. scales.
    c. paired fins.

_____ 5. The first vertebrates to evolve were
    a. amphibians.
    b. fishes.
    c. tunicates.

_____ 6. In fishes with gills, oxygen-rich water enters through the
    a. mouth and leaves through openings in the pharynx.
    b. mouth and leaves through the bladder.
    c. openings in the pharynx and leaves through the mouth.

_____ 7. Blood flows through the body of a fish in a
    a. single-loop, open circulatory system.
    b. single-loop, closed circulatory system.
    c. double-loop, open circulatory system.

_____ 8. The organ that adjusts the buoyancy of many bony fishes is the
    a. swim bladder.
    b. cerebellum.
    c. ventricle.

____ **9.** Modern jawless fishes include
   a. skates.
   b. sharks.
   c. lampreys.

____ **10.** All of the following are characteristics of most amphibians
   except
   a. they have scales and claws.
   b. they breathe with lungs as adults.
   c. they have moist skin that contains mucous glands.

____ **11.** The first amphibians probably resembled
   a. jawless fishes, like the lamprey.
   b. cartilaginous fishes, like the skate.
   c. lobe-finned fishes, like the coelacanth.

____ **12.** In the digestive system of a frog, where does food go after it
   leaves the mouth?
   a. to the gallbladder
   b. to the esophagus
   c. to the cloaca

____ **13.** In a frog, the cavity through which digestive wastes, urine,
   and eggs or sperm leave the body is the
   a. cloaca.
   b. colon.
   c. gallbladder.

____ **14.** The eggs of amphibians can dry out easily because they
   a. are never encased in jelly.
   b. do not have shells.
   c. are usually laid on land.

____ **15.** The amphibian in Figure 1 is a
   a. caecilian.
   b. frog.
   c. salamander.

Figure 1

Completion

Complete each statement on the line provided.

16. Individual segments of the backbone are called _____ .

17. The skeletons of some ancient fishes were made of _____ , which is
softer and more flexible than bone.

18. Adult salmon can distinguish their home stream from other streams by using their
sense of _____ .

19. The Carboniferous Period is sometimes referred to as the Age of _____ .

20. An adult amphibian's heart has _____ chambers.

Short Answer

In complete sentences, write the answers to the questions on the lines provided.

21. List the four characteristics of chordates.

_____

_____

_____

_____

22. How do lancelets move?

_____

_____

_____

_____

23. To which of the three main groups of fishes do each of the animals in Figure 2 belong?

_____

_____

_____

_____

24. List two adaptations of early amphibians that helped them live on land.

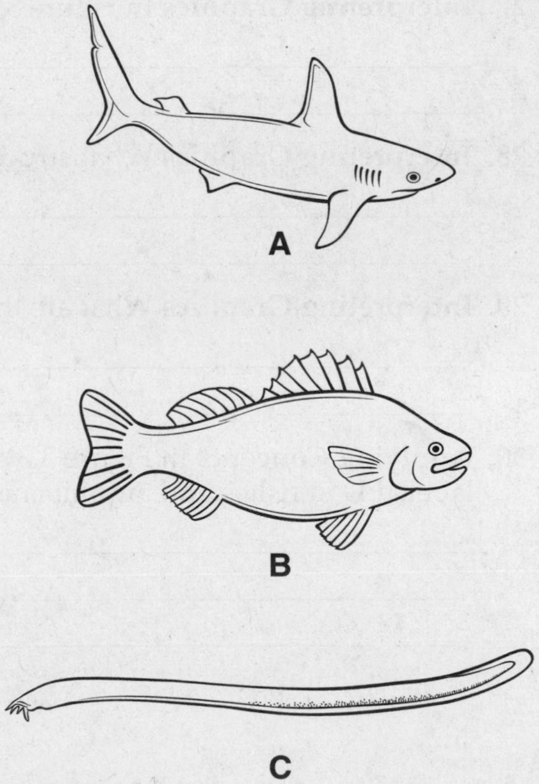

_____

_____

_____

_____

A

B

C

Figure 2

25. What are the three groups of modern amphibians?

_____

_____

_____

_____

Using Science Skills

Use the diagram below to answer the following questions on the lines provided.

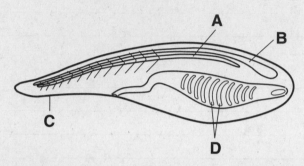

Figure 3

26. Interpreting Graphics In Figure 3, what is the structure labeled A?

_____

_____

27. Interpreting Graphics In Figure 3, what is the structure labeled B?

_____

_____

28. Interpreting Graphics What structure is labeled C in Figure 3?

_____

_____

29. Interpreting Graphics What are the structures labeled D in Figure 3?

_____

_____

30. Applying Concepts In Figure 3, what happens to the structures labeled D in fishes and amphibians?

_____

_____

_____

LESSON PLAN 31–1 (pages 797–805)

Reptiles

Time
2 periods
1 block

Section Objectives

- **31.1.1 Describe** the characteristics of reptiles.
- **31.1.2 Summarize** the evolution of reptiles.
- **31.1.3 Explain** how reptiles are adapted to life on land.
- **31.1.4 Identify** the four living orders of reptiles.

Vocabulary ectotherm • amniotic egg • carapace • plastron

Local Standards

---

1 FOCUS

Vocabulary Preview
Students infer the meaning of the word *ectotherm* from its word origins.

Targeted Resources
❏ Transparencies: **464** Section 31–1 Interest Grabber
❏ Transparencies: **465** Section 31–1 Outline

---

2 INSTRUCT

Build Science Skills: Comparing and Contrasting
Students make Venn diagrams to compare reptiles and amphibians. **L1** **L2**

Build Science Skills: Using Models
Students make a time line showing the sequence of events in reptile evolution. **L2**

Make Connections: Environmental Science
Discuss how climate changes affect plants and animals. **L2** **L3**

Demonstration
Students observe environmental differences in temperature to reinforce how ectotherms control body temperature. **L2**

Use Visuals: Figure 31–4
Use Figure 31–4 to review the reptilian circulatory system. **L1** **L2**

Build Science Skills: Using Models
Students create their own reptile. **L2**

Targeted Resources
❏ Reading and Study Workbook: Section 31–1
❏ Adapted Reading and Study Workbook: Section 31–1
❏ Teaching Resources: Section Summaries 31–1, Worksheets 31–1
❏ Transparencies: **466** Structure of a Turtle's Heart, **467** Figure 31–8 The Amniotic Egg
❏ Lab Manual A: Chapter 31 Lab
❏ **NSTA** *sci*LINKS Dinosaur extinction

---

3 ASSESS

Evaluate Understanding
Play a quiz game in which you give students answers about reptiles and they give you the questions.

Reteach
Students diagram the main characteristics of reptiles.

Targeted Resources
❏ Teaching Resources: Section Review 31–1
❏ **iText** Section 31–1

LESSON PLAN 31–2 (pages 806–814)

Birds

Section Objectives   Local Standards

- **31.2.1 Describe** the characteristics of all birds.
- **31.2.2 Summarize** the evolution of birds.
- **31.2.3 Explain** how birds are adapted for flight.
- **31.2.4 Describe** the diversity of birds.
- **31.2.5 Identify** ways in which birds interact with the environment and with humans.

Vocabulary feather • endotherm • crop • gizzard • air sac

1 FOCUS

Reading Strategy
Students preview Figure 31–14 to identify the characteristics of birds.

Targeted Resources
❑ Transparencies: **468** Section 31–2 Interest Grabber, **469** Section 31–2 Outline, **470** Concept Map

2 INSTRUCT

Use Visuals: Figure 31–11
Students compare and contrast the feather structures illustrated in Figure 31–11. **L1 L2**

Build Science Skills: Inferring
Students infer the kind of fossil evidence that would show that birds and dinosaurs evolved from a common ancestor. **L2 L3**

Quick Lab
Students use models to explain how birds breathe. **L2**

Make Connections: Physics
Students experiment with different wing shapes to produce flight. **L2**

Address Misconceptions
Explain how birds really flap their wings. **L2**

Build Science Skills: Classifying
Students use their own criteria to divide birds into different groups. **L1 L2**

Targeted Resources
❑ Reading and Study Workbook: Section 31–2
❑ Adapted Reading and Study Workbook: Section 31–2
❑ Transparencies: **471** Figure 31–14 The Digestive System of a Pigeon, **472** Figure 31–16 The Structure of a Bird's Heart
❑ Teaching Resources: Section Summaries 31–2, Worksheets 31–2, Enrichment
❑ Lab Worksheets: Chapter 31 Exploration
❑ Lab Manual B: Chapter 31 Lab
❑ **NSTA** sc*i*_{LINKS} Birds

3 ASSESS

Evaluate Understanding
Quiz students orally about the characteristics and adaptations of birds.

Reteach
Students use Figures 31–11, 31–14, and 31–19 to review characteristics of birds.

Targeted Resources
❑ Teaching Resources: Section Review 31–2, Chapter Vocabulary Review, Graphic Organizer, Chapter 31 Tests: Levels A and B
❑ **iText** Section 31–2, Chapter 31 Assessment
❑ **PHSchool.com** Online Chapter 31 Test

Chapter 31   Reptiles and Birds

Summary

31–1 Reptiles

At the end of the Carboniferous Period, the climate became drier. Amphibians began dying out. This led to new habitats for reptiles. The Mesozoic Era is called the Age of Reptiles because of the diversity and large numbers of reptiles that lived during that period. Dinosaurs were everywhere. The Age of Reptiles ended with a mass extinction at the end of the Cretaceous Period.

Reptiles are vertebrates adapted for life on land. They have several adaptations that make them better able to survive on land than amphibians. Reptiles have dry skin covered by protective scales. The scales help hold water in their bodies. **They have well-developed lungs. Reptiles also have eggs with a shell and several membranes.**

Most reptiles have adapted to a fully terrestrial life.

- Body Temperature Control. Reptiles are **ectotherms.** Their body temperature is controlled by behavior. To warm up, they bask in the sun. To cool down, they move into shade, burrow underground, or go for a swim.
- Feeding. Reptiles eat many foods and have many different ways of eating. Some reptiles are herbivores, others are carnivores.
- Respiration. The lungs of reptiles are better developed than those of amphibians. Reptile lungs have more gas-exchange area than those of amphibians. Muscles around a reptile's ribs allow the animal to expand its chest to inhale and collapse its chest to exhale. Although most reptiles have two lungs, some snakes have only one lung.
- Circulation. Reptiles have a double-loop circulatory system. One loop carries blood to and from the lungs. The other carries blood to and from the rest of the body. Most reptiles have a three-chambered heart. Crocodiles have two atria and two ventricles.
- Excretion. Reptiles get rid of liquid wastes as urine. In some reptiles, urine flows directly into a cloaca. In other reptiles, a urinary bladder stores urine. Reptiles that live mainly in water excrete ammonia. Those living on land convert ammonia to uric acid. Uric acid is less toxic than ammonia and less water is required to dilute it. By eliminating wastes that contain little water, a reptile can conserve water.
- Response. The cerebrum and cerebellum are larger in reptile brains than in amphibian brains. Reptiles have well-developed sense organs.

- <u>Movement</u>. Reptiles have larger and stronger limbs than amphibians. In most reptiles, the legs are rotated under the body. This allows the legs to carry more body weight.
- <u>Reproduction</u>. Reptiles have internal fertilization. Most are oviparous, laying eggs that develop outside the mother's body. The embryos are covered with membranes and a protective shell. This type of egg, called an **amniotic egg** keeps the embryo from drying out. The amniotic egg is one of the most important adaptations to life on land. Some snakes and lizards are ovoviviparous—their young are born alive.

Four groups of reptiles survive today:
- **Lizards and snakes** Most lizards have legs, clawed toes, external ears, and movable eyelids. Snakes are legless.
- **Crocodilians** have long, broad snouts and a squat appearance. They are fierce carnivores that live only in tropical climates. Crocodilians include alligators, crocodiles, caimans, and gavials.
- **Turtles and tortoises** have backbones fused to a protective shell. Turtles usually live in water. Tortoises usually live on land. Instead of teeth, these reptiles have horny ridges on their jaws.
- The **tuatara** lives only on a few islands near New Zealand. They look somewhat like lizards, but lack external ears and have primitive scales. They also have a "third eye," which is part of a sense organ on the top of the brain.

31–2 Birds

Birds are reptilelike animals that maintain a constant internal body temperature. Birds have two legs covered with scales. Their front legs are modified into wings. Birds are covered with feathers. Feathers help most birds fly and stay warm.

Paleontologists agree that birds evolved from reptiles that are now extinct. Some think that birds evolved directly from dinosaurs. Others think that birds and dinosaurs evolved from an earlier common ancestor.

Birds have a number of adaptations that enable them to fly. These include highly efficient digestive, respiratory, and circulatory systems; aerodynamic feathers and wings; strong, lightweight bones; and strong chest muscles.
- <u>Body Temperature Control</u>. Birds have a high metabolic rate that produces heat. Animals that generate their own heat are called **endotherms.** A bird's feathers help conserve this heat. To maintain a high metabolic rate, birds need to eat large amounts of food. The beaks of birds are adapted to the type of food they eat.

- Feeding. Some birds have digestive organs called a crop and a gizzard. The **crop,** located at the end of the esophagus, stores and moistens food. The **gizzard** is part of the stomach. It grinds and crushes food.
- Respiration. Birds have a very efficient respiratory system. Birds can remove oxygen from air both when they inhale and when they exhale. They can do this because their lungs are connected at the front and back to large air sacs. Air flows into the air sacs and out through the lungs in one direction. The lungs are always exposed to oxygen-rich air.
- Circulation. Birds have a four-chambered heart and two circulatory loops. A bird's heart has two separate ventricles. Oxygen-rich blood and oxygen-poor blood are completely separated.
- Excretion. Birds have an excretory system similar to that of reptiles. Nitrogen wastes are changed to uric acid and sent to the cloaca. The cloaca reabsorbs water from the wastes, which are then expelled.
- Response. Birds have a well-developed brain and sense organs. The cerebrum and cerebellum are large in relation to body size. These adaptations help birds respond quickly to stimuli and coordinate the movements for flight. Birds have well-developed sight and hearing, but do not smell or taste well.
- Movement. The bodies, wings, legs, and feet of birds are adapted to different habitats and lifestyles. Some of these adaptations, such as air spaces in bones, help birds fly. However, not all birds fly.
- Reproduction. Birds have internal fertilization. They lay amniotic eggs with hard shells. Most birds keep their eggs warm until they hatch. One or both parents may then care for the offspring.

Reptilian Heart

The reptilian heart is made up of three chambers: two atria and one partially divided ventricle.

Color the blood vessels and chambers of the heart according to the prompts below.

- Color the areas that hold oxygen-rich blood red.
- Color the areas that hold oxygen-poor blood blue.

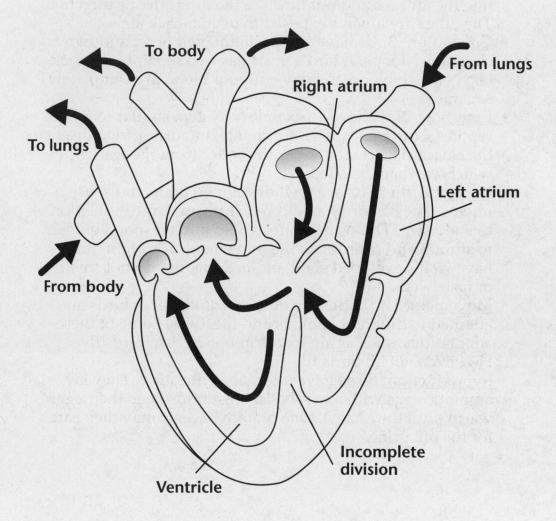

Use the diagram to answer the questions.

1. In which chamber do oxygen-rich blood and oxygen-poor blood mix?

_____

2. From where does the heart get oxygen-rich blood?

_____

Amniotic Egg

The amniotic egg is an important adaptation for reptiles. It prevents the embryo from drying out. It allows reptiles to lay their eggs on land.

Color the diagram of an amniotic egg according to the prompts.
- Color the amnion orange.
- Color the chorion red.
- Color the yolk sac yellow.
- Color the allantois green.

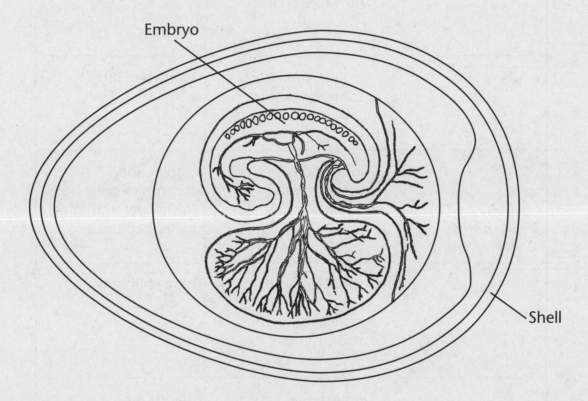

Embryo

Shell

Use the diagram to answer the questions.

1. Which structure stores the embryo's waste? Circle the correct answer.

allantois   chorion

2. What is the function of the amnion?

_____

_____

Types of Reptiles

Some characteristics of tuataras, crocodilians, snakes, lizards, *and* turtles and tortoises *are described below. Use what you know about reptiles to complete the table. One row has been done for you.*

Reptile	Typical Features	Where Found
lizards	legs, clawed toes; external ears; movable eyelids	many habitats
	legless; predators, some venomous	many habitats
	long and typically broad snout; carnivores	tropics and subtropics only; both freshwater and salt-water habitats
	shell built into skeleton; horny ridges instead of teeth; strong limbs	many habitats
	no external ears; primitive scales; "third eye" that senses sunlight	islands off New Zealand only

Use the table to answer the questions.

1. Which reptiles are legless?

_____

2. Which reptiles have a "third eye" that senses light?

_____

Feathers

Feathers make up the outer covering of birds. There are two main types of feathers: contour feathers and down feathers.

Circle the contour feather in red. Circle the down feather in blue.

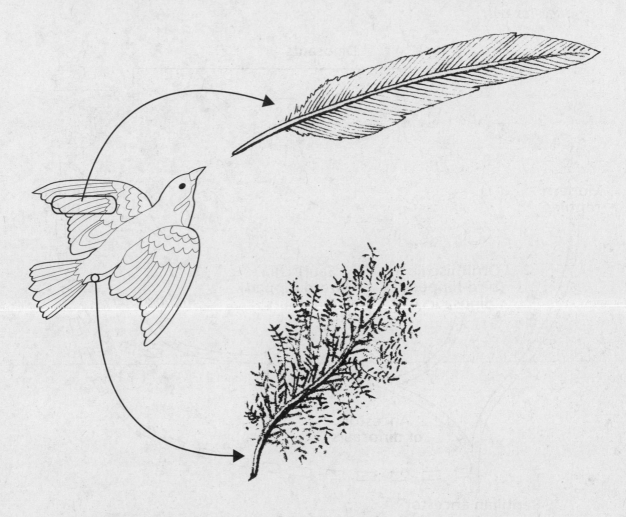

Answer the questions.

1. What is the function of contour feathers?

_____

2. What is the function of down feathers?

_____

Bird Evolution

Modern scientists are not sure how birds evolved. The cladogram below shows two theories of bird evolution.

Color the path that shows birds evolving directly from dinosaurs blue. Color the path that shows birds and dinosaurs sharing an earlier common ancestor red.

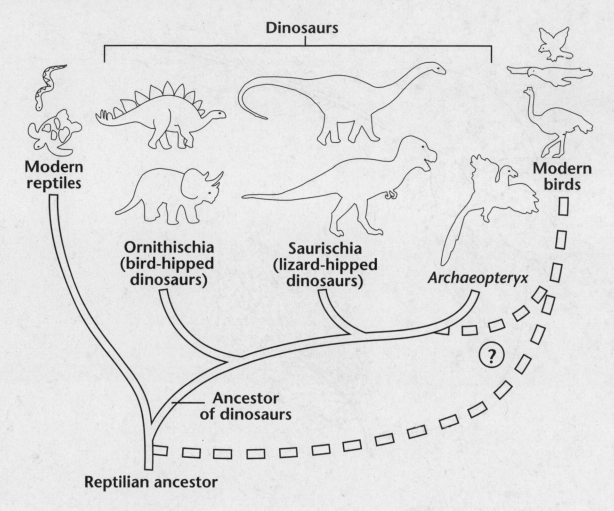

Answer the questions.

1. How does *Archaeopteryx* provide evidence to support the theory that birds evolved from dinosaurs?

_____

_____

_____

2. Which of the following characteristics do modern birds and living reptiles share? Circle the correct answer.

   amniotic eggs   feathers

Bird Heart

The bird heart is made up of four chambers: the right atrium, left atrium, right ventricle and left ventricle.

Color the blood vessels and areas of the heart that hold oxygen-rich blood red. Color the areas that hold oxygen-poor blood blue.

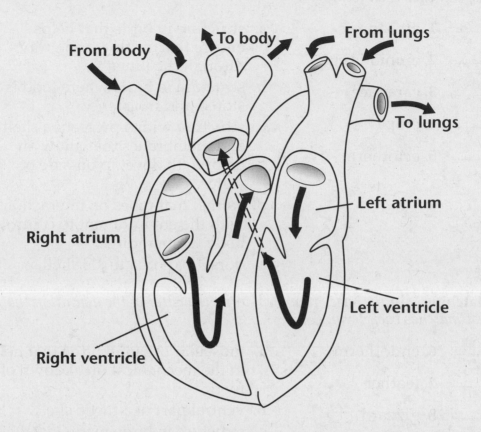

Use the diagram to answer the questions.

1. From where does the heart receive oxygen-poor blood?

_____

_____

2. How is a bird heart different from a reptile heart?

_____

_____

Chapter 31   Reptiles and Birds

Vocabulary Review

Matching   *In the space provided, write the letter of the definition that best matches each term.*

_____ **1.** air sac

_____ **2.** amniotic egg

_____ **3.** carapace

_____ **4.** crop

_____ **5.** ectotherm

a. structure in birds that helps ensure that air flows one way through the lungs

b. structure in birds where food is stored and moistened

c. structure with a protective shell and membranes that allow an embryo to develop outside of water

d. animal that relies on interactions with the environment to control body temperature

e. dorsal part of a turtle shell

Matching   *In the space provided, write the letter of the definition that best matches each term.*

_____ **6.** endotherm

_____ **7.** feather

_____ **8.** gizzard

_____ **9.** plastron

a. muscular organ in birds that helps in the mechanical breakdown of food

b. ventral part of a turtle shell

c. structure in birds made mostly of protein that can aid in flight and temperature control

d. animal that generates its own body heat

Name_____ Class_____ Date _____

Summary

31–1 Reptiles

Reptiles are vertebrates that are adapted to live entirely on land. They have dry skin that is covered with protective scales. This helps hold water in their bodies. They have efficient lungs that get oxygen from air. Reptiles also have eggs with a shell and several membranes.

As the climate became drier at the end of the Carboniferous Period, amphibians began dying out. This opened up many new habitats for reptiles. The Mesozoic Era is often called the Age of Reptiles because of the diversity and large numbers of reptiles that lived. Dinosaurs were everywhere. The Age of Reptiles ended with a mass extinction at the end of the Cretaceous Period.

Reptiles are ectotherms. They control their body temperature by their behavior. To warm up, they bask in the sun. To cool down, they move into shade, go for a swim, or move to an underground burrow.

Reptiles eat a wide range of foods. They also have many different ways of eating.

Reptile lungs have more gas-exchange area than amphibian lungs. Reptiles also have muscles around their ribs. They are able to expand their chest to inhale and collapse it to exhale.

Reptiles have a double-loop circulatory system. One loop carries blood to and from the lungs. The other loop carries blood to and from the rest of the body. Most reptiles have a three-chambered heart with a partially separated ventricle. Crocodiles have two atria and two ventricles.

Reptiles get rid of liquid wastes as urine. The urine contains either ammonia or uric acid. Reptiles that live in water excrete ammonia. Reptiles that live on land convert ammonia to uric acid. Uric acid is less toxic and requires less water to dilute it.

The reptilian brain is similar to the amphibian brain. However, the cerebrum and cerebellum are larger. Reptiles have well-developed sense organs.

Reptiles have larger and stronger limbs than amphibians. Their legs are rotated further under the body than those of amphibians. In this position, the legs can carry more body weight.

Reptiles have internal fertilization. Most are oviparous, laying eggs that develop outside the mother's body. The embryos are covered with membranes and a protective shell. This amniotic egg keeps the embryo from drying out. Some snakes and lizards are ovoviviparous, and the young are born alive.

Four groups of reptiles survive today. Lizards and snakes (order Squamata) have legs, clawed toes, external ears, and movable eyelids. Snakes are lizards that have lost their legs during their evolution.

Crocodilians (order Crocodilia) have long, broad snouts and a squat appearance. They are fierce carnivores that live only in tropical climates. Crocodilians include alligators, crocodiles, caimans, and gavials.

Turtles and tortoises (order Testudines) have backbones fused to a shell, which provides protection. Turtles usually live in water. Tortoises usually live on land. Instead of teeth, these reptiles have horny ridges on their jaws.

The tuatara (order Sphenodonta) is found only on a few islands near New Zealand. They look somewhat like lizards, but do not have external ears and have primitive scales. They also have a "third eye," which is part of a sense organ on the top of the brain.

31–2 Birds

Birds are reptilelike animals that have a constant internal body temperature. They have two legs that are covered with scales. Their front legs are modified into wings. Birds are covered with feathers. Feathers help birds fly and keep them warm. Birds have different kinds of feathers.

Paleontologists agree that birds evolved from extinct reptiles. Some think that birds evolved directly from dinosaurs. Others think that birds and dinosaurs evolved from an earlier common ancestor.

Birds have many adaptations that enable them to fly. Birds are endotherms. They produce their own body heat. Their high metabolic rate produces heat. Feathers help conserve this heat.

Birds need to eat large amounts of food to maintain their high metabolic rate. Birds have bills adapted to the type of food they eat. Some birds have digestive organs called a crop and a gizzard. The crop is located at the end of the esophagus. Food is stored and moistened in the crop. The gizzard is part of the stomach. It grinds and crushes food so that it is easier to digest.

Birds have a very efficient respiratory system. A system of air sacs and breathing tubes ensures that air flows into the air sacs and out through the lungs in one direction. The lungs are constantly exposed to oxygen-rich air. This helps birds maintain their high metabolic rate.

Birds have a four-chambered heart and two circulatory loops. A bird's heart has two separate ventricles. Oxygen-rich blood and oxygen-poor blood are completely separated.

Birds have an excretory system similar to that of reptiles. Nitrogenous wastes are converted to uric acid and sent to the cloaca. The cloaca reabsorbs most of the water from the wastes before they are expelled.

Birds have a well-developed brain and sense organs. The cerebrum and cerebellum are large in relation to body size. These adaptations enable birds to respond quickly to stimuli and coordinate the movements for flight. Birds have well-developed sight and hearing but do not sense smells or tastes very well.

The bodies, wings, legs, and feet of birds are adapted to many different habitats and lifestyles. Some of these adaptations, like air spaces in bones, help birds fly. All birds, however, do not fly.

Birds have internal fertilization. They lay amniotic eggs that have a hard shell. Most birds keep their eggs warm until they hatch. One or both parents may care for the offspring.

Section 31–1 Reptiles (pages 797–805)

Key Concepts

- What are the characteristics of reptiles?
- How are reptiles adapted to life on land?
- What are the four living orders of reptiles?

What Is a Reptile? (page 797)

1. List three characteristics shared by all reptiles.

   a. _____

   b. _____

   c. _____

2. What is the disadvantage of reptilian scaly skin? _____

   _____

   _____

Evolution of Reptiles (pages 798–799)

3. Circle the letter of each sentence that is true about the evolution of reptiles.

   a. Reptiles evolved rapidly in the warm, humid climate of the Carboniferous Period.

   b. Mammal-like reptiles dominated many land habitats until near the end of the Triassic Period.

   c. All dinosaurs were enormous.

   d. Some dinosaurs may have had feathers.

4. Is the following sentence true or false? The extinction of dinosaurs opened up new niches on land and in the sea, providing opportunities for other kinds of organisms to evolve.

   _____

Form and Function in Reptiles (pages 800–802)

5. How do ectotherms control their body temperature? _____

   _____

   _____

6. Is the following sentence true or false? All reptiles are herbivores. _____

7. Circle the letter of each adaptation reptiles have for respiration.

   a. lungs   c. strong rib muscles

   b. moist skin   d. gill slits

8. Circle the letter of each sentence that is true about circulation in reptiles.

   a. Reptiles have a double-loop circulatory system.

   b. All reptile hearts have only one atrium.

   c. Most reptiles have one ventricle with partial internal walls.

   d. Crocodiles have the least developed heart of living reptiles.

9. What is the advantage of uric acid to terrestrial reptiles? _____
_____
_____

10. Circle the letter of each sentence that is true about response in reptiles.

   a. The reptilian cerebrum is smaller than that of amphibians.

   b. Reptiles that are active during the day tend to have complex eyes.

   c. Reptiles do not have ears.

   d. Snakes sense vibrations in the ground through bones in their skulls.

11. Explain why reptiles are able to carry more body weight than amphibians.
_____
_____

12. All reptiles reproduce by _____ fertilization in which the male deposits sperm inside the body of the female.

13. In the diagram below, label the four membranes in the amniotic egg that surround the developing embryo.

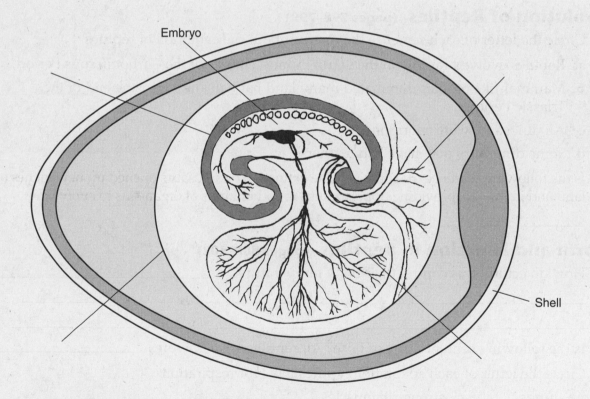

Embryo

Shell

Groups of Reptiles (pages 803–805)

14. What are the four living orders of reptiles?
_____
_____

15. Is the following sentence true or false? Both snakes and lizards have scaly skin and clawed toes. _____

16. Circle the letter of each characteristic of crocodilians.

    a. long snout   **c.** herbivore

    b. long legs   **d.** protective of young

17. Members of the order Testudines that live on land are referred to as

_____.

18. How do most turtles and tortoises protect themselves? _____

_____

19. Circle the letter of each characteristic of turtles and tortoises.

    a. teeth   **c.** strong limbs

    b. strong jaws   **d.** long, broad snout

20. Describe how tuataras differ from lizards. _____

_____

_____

Ecology of Reptiles (page 805)

21. Circle the letter of each sentence that is true about the ecology of reptiles.

    a. Reptiles are in no danger of disappearing.

    b. Reptilian habitats have been expanding.

    c. Humans hunt reptiles for food, to sell as pets, and for their skins.

    d. Conservation programs are in place to help reptiles survive.

Reading Skill Practice

Flowcharts can help you to order the steps in a process or the stages in a series of events. Construct a flowchart that shows the stages in the evolution of reptiles, beginning at the end of the Carboniferous Period and ending with the extinction of dinosaurs at the end of the Cretaceous Period. See Appendix A in your textbook for more information about flowcharts. Do your work on a separate sheet of paper.

Section 31–2 Birds (pages 806–814)

 Key Concepts
- What characteristics do birds have in common?
- How are birds adapted for flight?

What Is a Bird? (page 806)

1. Circle the letter of each characteristic of birds.

   a. feathers

   b. four legs

   c. wings

   d. scales

2. The single most important characteristic that separates birds from all other living

   animals is _____.

3. List two functions of feathers.

   a. _____

   b. _____

4. Identify each type of feather diagrammed below.

   _____   _____

Evolution of Birds (page 807)

5. In what ways is the early bird *Archaeopteryx* different from modern birds?

   _____

   _____

6. Is the following sentence true or false? Scientists know for certain that birds evolved

   directly from dinosaurs. _____

Form, Function, and Flight (pages 808–812)

7. What adaptations do birds have that enable them to fly? _____

_____

_____

_____

8. For what two things do birds require energy?

a. _____

b. _____

9. Is the following sentence true or false? Birds have a low metabolic rate compared to reptiles. _____

Match the type of bird bill with the type of food it is adapted to eat.

	Bird Bill	**Food**
_____	**10.** Short and fine	**a.** Flower nectar
_____	**11.** Short and thick	**b.** Seeds
_____	**12.** Strong and hooked	**c.** Insects
_____	**13.** Long and thin	**d.** Animal prey

14. What is the main function of the crop? _____

_____

15. Why might a bird swallow gravel or small stones? _____

_____

_____

16. What is an advantage of the one-way airflow through a bird's lungs? _____

_____

_____

17. What type of circulatory system do birds have? _____

_____

18. Circle the letter of the form of nitrogenous waste excreted by birds.

a. ammonia

b. urea

c. uric acid

d. nitrate

19. Circle the letter of each sentence that is true about response in birds.

    a. Birds have brains that quickly interpret and respond to signals.

    b. The cerebrum controls behaviors, such as nest building.

    c. The cerebellum in birds is much like that in reptiles.

    d. Birds can sense tastes and smells quite well.

20. What are two ways in which the skeleton of a flying bird is strengthened for flight?

    a. _____

    b. _____

21. How are the amniotic eggs of birds different from the eggs of reptiles? _____

_____

_____

22. Is the following sentence true or false? Bird parents do not ever care for their offspring.

_____

Groups of Birds (pages 812–813)

Match the bird group with its characteristics. Use Figure 31–19 as a guide.

Bird Groups	Characteristics
_____ 23. Birds of prey	**a.** Largest order of birds, which includes songbirds
_____ 24. Ostriches and their relatives	**b.** Fierce predators with hooked bills, large wingspans, and sharp talons
_____ 25. Parrots	**c.** Flightless birds that move by running
_____ 26. Perching birds	**d.** Adapted to wading in aquatic habitats
_____ 27. Herons and their relatives	**e.** Colorful, noisy birds that use their feet to hold up food
_____ 28. Cavity-nesting birds	**f.** Birds found in all types of aquatic ecosystems; have four toes connected by a web
_____ 29. Pelicans and their relatives	**g.** Multicolored birds that live in holes made in trees, mounds, or underground tunnels

Ecology of Birds (page 814)

30. Circle the letter of each way in which birds interact with natural ecosystems.

    a. pollinate flowers

    b. disperse seeds

    c. control insects

    d. produce toxic wastes

31. Is the following sentence true or false? Some species of migrating birds use stars and other celestial bodies as guides. _____

32. Is the following sentence true or false? Birds are not affected by changes in the environment. _____

Reading Skill Practice

By looking at illustrations in textbooks, you can help yourself remember better what you have read. Look carefully at Figure 31–14 on page 809 in your textbook. What important information does the illustration communicate? Do your work on a separate sheet of paper.

Chapter 31 Reptiles and Birds

Vocabulary Review

Matching *In the space provided, write the letter of the definition that best matches each term.*

_____ **1.** ectotherms

_____ **2.** endotherms

_____ **3.** carapace

_____ **4.** plastron

_____ **5.** crop

_____ **6.** gizzard

a. digestive structure that grinds and crushes food

b. animals that can generate their own body heat

c. animals that rely on behavior to control body temperature

d. ventral part of a turtle shell

e. dorsal part of a turtle shell

f. digestive structure that stores and moistens food

Completion *Fill in the blanks with terms from Chapter 31.*

7. One of the most important adaptations to life on land is the _____, which protects the growing embryo and keeps it from drying out.

8. An outer covering of _____ helps birds fly and keeps them warm.

9. In birds, _____ direct air through the lungs in an efficient, one-way flow.

Labeling Diagrams *Use the following words to label the amniotic egg:* allantois, amnion, chorion, embryo, shell, *and* yolk sac.

10. _____

15. _____

11. _____

14. _____

12. _____

13. _____

Chapter 31 Reptiles and Birds   **Section Review 31-1**

Reviewing Key Concepts

Identification *On the lines provided, write* Yes *if the characteristic describes a reptile, and write* No *if it does not.*

_____ 1 lungs used for breathing

_____ 2. shelled eggs

_____ 3. double-loop circulatory system

_____ 4. inefficient excretory system

_____ 5. weak limbs

_____ 6. internal fertilization

_____ 7. constant internal body temperature

Completion *On the lines provided, identify the group of reptiles—Lizards and snakes, Tuataras, Crocodilians, or Turtles and tortoises—that best completes the sentence.*

8. _____ have shells built into their skeletons.

9. _____ have long, broad snouts and a squat appearance.

10. _____ have clawed toes, external ears, and movable eyelids.

11. _____ are found only on a few islands near New Zealand.

Short Answer *On the lines provided, answer the following:*

12. Describe the excretory system of reptiles that live on land.

_____

_____

13. Explain an advantage and a disadvantage of a reptile's scaly skin.

_____

_____

Reviewing Key Skills

14. **Interpreting Graphics** Name the four membranes in the amniotic egg and give their functions.

_____

_____

_____

15. **Comparing and Contrasting** Describe the similarities and differences between the ways in which reptiles and amphibians move on land.

_____

_____

_____

Name_____ Class_____ Date _____

Reviewing Key Concepts

Completion *On the lines provided, complete the following sentences.*

1. Birds have a (an) _____ internal body temperature.

2. A bird's outer covering of _____ sets it apart
   from all other animals.

3. The strong _____ muscles of a bird power the wing strokes
   for flight.

Identification *On the lines provided, identify each adaptation in a bird shown
here, and explain why it enables a bird to fly.*

4. _____

   _____

5. _____

   _____

Short Answer *On the lines provided, answer the following questions.*

6. What features of a bird's circulatory system improve its ability to fly?

   _____

   _____

7. Describe the respiratory system of birds and how it is adapted for flight.

   _____

   _____

Reviewing Key Skills

8. **Comparing and Contrasting** Give three examples of how birds'
   beaks or bills are adapted to the type of food they eat.

   _____

   _____

9. **Applying Concepts** A student noticed a particular bird that ate mostly
   insects and seeds. Do you think this bird has a gizzard? Explain your answer.

   _____

   _____

10. **Inferring** Hooks on the barbules of contour feathers hold the barbules
    together and keep them flat. How is this an advantage for flight?

    _____

    _____

Name_____ Class_____ Date _____

Crossword Puzzle *Use the clues below to complete the puzzle.*

Across

1. organ in which food is stored and moistened (in birds)

3. dorsal part of a turtle's shell

7. type of egg composed of a shell and membranes that creates a protected environment in which the embryo can develop without drying out

8. typical bird structure; helps birds fly and keeps them warm

Down

2. ventral part of a turtle's shell

4. where air first enters when a bird inhales (two words)

5. animal that can generate its own body heat

6. in a bird, the organ that helps in the mechanical breakdown of food

9. animal that relies on interactions with the environment to control body temperature

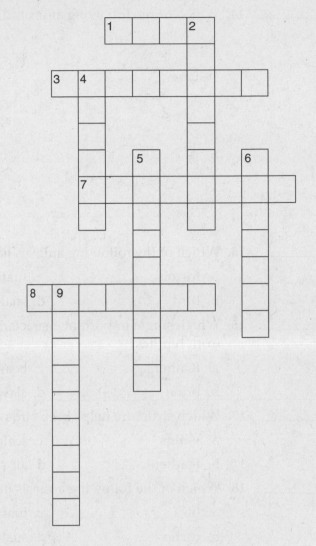

Multiple Choice *On the lines provided, write the letter that best completes the sentence or answers the question.*

_____ **10.** A turtle is an example of a(an)

    a. endotherm.   c. amphibian.

    b. ectotherm.   d. mammal.

_____ **11.** What does an ectotherm use to warm up?

    a. down feathers   c. the sun

    b. contour feathers   d. fur

_____ **12.** One of the most important adaptations to life on land is the

    a. ability to fly.   c. ability to hunt.

    b. crop.   d. amniotic egg.

_____ 13. Which of the following animals does NOT produce an amniotic egg?

   a. turtle   c. frog

   b. snake   d. tuatara

_____ 14. Which of the following animals has a carapace?

   a.   c.

   b.   d.

_____ 15. Which of the following animals has a plastron?

   a. tortoise   c. tuatara

   b. bird   d. snake

_____ 16. Which single important characteristic separates birds from reptiles?

   a. feather   c. beak

   b. brain   d. claw

_____ 17. Which structure helps keep birds warm?

   a. wings   c. scales

   b. feathers   d. air sacs

_____ 18. Which of the following animals has a crop?

   a. bird   c. tuatara

   b. turtle   d. snake

_____ 19. What structure in a bird contains small bits of gravel?

   a. air sac   c. plastron

   b. amniotic egg   d. gizzard

_____ 20. The structures that allow for the one-way airflow through a bird's respiratory system are

   a. beaks.   c. crops.

   b. gizzards.   d. air sacs.

Bird Migration

Some birds stay in one place all year. However, most species of birds migrate, or move from one location to another with the changing seasons. Some migrate over short distances, and some migrate over very long distances. House sparrows remain in their home areas all year. The American robin migrates south only as far as it must to find food, and it may not migrate at all if food remains plentiful all year in its summer quarters. In contrast, the Arctic tern migrates from the far north to the Antarctic every year, flying almost halfway around the world.

Many ducks are long-distance migrants. Blue-winged teals migrate more than 9600 km, from 60° N latitude in North America to below 30° S in South America. Northern shovelers migrate up to 11,000 km.

Migration requires an enormous amount of energy, and many birds die as they travel between their winter and summer homes. But birds have much to gain from migration. Migration allows birds to take advantage of resources that exist for only part of the year. Migratory birds may nest in the northern tundra during the summer when temperatures are warm and food is plentiful, then move south again before the onset of winter.

The migration of cranes has been observed by humans since ancient times. In Japan, the cranes return to the same rice paddies every winter. They are strictly protected by the Japanese farmers, who consider the birds an auspicious sign of the coming spring. Another species of crane, called the whooping crane, lives in North America. The whooping crane is an endangered species, with very few left in the wild. Wild whooping cranes spend the winter along the Texas Gulf coast and breed in Alberta, Canada.

How do birds know when to migrate? The timing of the long-distance migrations is built into the birds' hormonal cycles. Birds have "annual clocks" that are synchronized to length of daylight and climatic changes. When the air pressure systems create a beneficial airflow, birds begin their migration. During the flight, bad weather conditions may cause a temporary layover. When conditions improve, the birds move on. Scientists think that birds navigate using the sun, stars, landmarks, and even Earth's magnetic field.

Evaluation *On the lines provided, answer the following questions.*

1. Do all birds migrate? Explain your answer.

   _____

   _____

2. What are some advantages and disadvantages of migration?

   _____

   _____

3. How do birds know when to migrate? Explain your answer.

   _____

   _____

Chapter 31 Reptiles and Birds   **Graphic Organizer**

Concept Map

Using information from the chapter, complete the concept map below. If there is not enough room in the concept map to write your answers, write them on a separate sheet of paper.

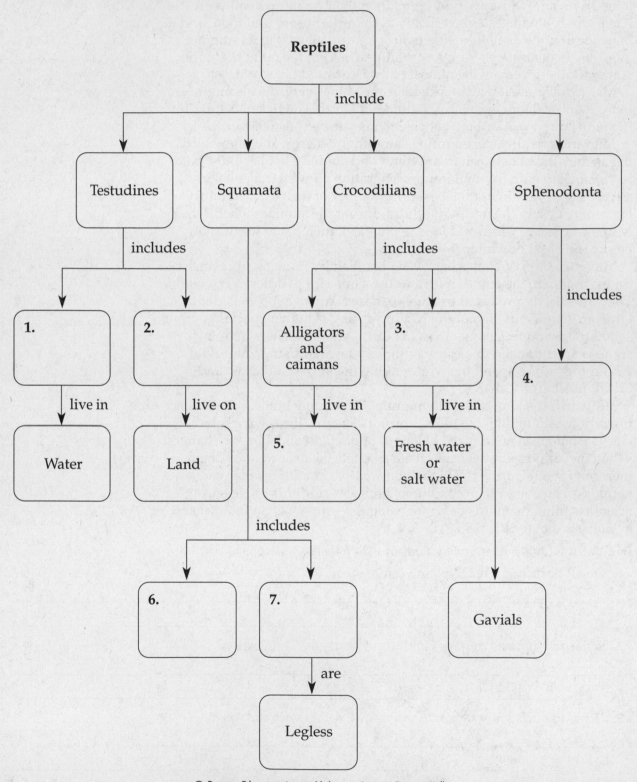

Chapter 31 Reptiles and Birds | **Chapter Test A**

Multiple Choice

Write the letter that best answers the question or completes the statement on the line provided.

_____ 1. Reptile hearts contain
   a. one atrium and one ventricle.
   b. one atrium and either one or two ventricles.
   c. two atria and two ventricles.
   d. two atria and either one or two ventricles.

_____ 2. One reason for the first great adaptive radiation of reptiles was that
   a. reptiles could reproduce without water.
   b. reptiles were strictly aquatic.
   c. Earth's climate became warmer and more humid.
   d. lakes and swamps became more numerous.

_____ 3. One characteristic that all reptiles share is
   a. a similar body size.
   b. the number of legs they used for moving around on land.
   c. what they eat.
   d. how the embryos develop.

_____ 4. Which of the following is NOT an adaptation for a completely terrestrial life?
   a. limb girdles
   b. lungs
   c. scaly skin
   d. amniotic egg

_____ 5. Compared with the limbs of most amphibians, the limbs of reptiles tend to be
   a. smaller and weaker.
   b. capable of carrying less weight.
   c. located farther under the body.
   d. less specialized in form and function.

_____ 6. All reptiles reproduce by
   a. internal fertilization, and most are oviparous.
   b. internal fertilization, and most are viviparous.
   c. external fertilization, and most are viviparous.
   d. external fertilization, and all are ovoviviparous.

_____ 7. A four-chambered heart is found in
   a. tuataras.   c. turtles.
   b. snakes.   d. alligators.

____ **8.** Caimans and gavials belong to the order
 a. Squamata.   c. Testudines.
 b. Crocodilia.   d. Rhynchocephalia.

____ **9.** What is the order in which food passes through the digestive system of a seed-eating bird?
 a. large intestine → crop → stomach → small intestine
 b. stomach → large intestine → crop → small intestine
 c. crop → stomach → small intestine → large intestine
 d. crop → large intestine → small intestine → stomach

____ **10.** Which of the following statements about temperature regulation in birds is NOT correct?
 a. Birds are endotherms.
 b. A bird's body temperature depends on the temperature of the outside environment.
 c. Bird's can generate their own body heat.
 d. Feathers help birds conserve body heat.

____ **11.** The main function of contour feathers is to
 a. trap air close to a bird's body.
 b. provide the lifting force and balance needed for flight.
 c. make a bird's respiratory system more efficient.
 d. release a powder that repels water.

____ **12.** A bird's respiratory system is more efficient than that of other land vertebrates because
 a. inhaled air passes directly into the lungs.
 b. oxygen-poor air is inhaled along with oxygen-rich air.
 c. air flows through the lungs in only one direction.
 d. none of the space in the lungs is occupied by tubes.

____ **13.** The structure of a bird's heart ensures that
 a. oxygen-rich blood never mixes with oxygen-poor blood.
 b. oxygen-rich blood is always pumped to the lungs.
 c. oxygen-poor blood is always pumped to the body.
 d. oxygen-poor blood never enters the heart.

____ **14.** If a bird has a hooked bill and sharp talons, it might be a(an)
 a. water bird.   c. bird of prey.
 b. ostrich.   d. perching bird.

____ **15.** Which of the following is NOT a likely mechanism by which migrating birds find their way?
 a. using stars as guides
 b. following landmarks
 c. following the scent of certain flowers
 d. sensing Earth's magnetic field

Name______________________________ Class__________________ Date ______________

Completion

Complete each statement on the line provided.

16. A mass ________________ at the end of the Cretaceous Period was caused by a series of natural disasters and marked the end of the dinosaurs.

17. An egg in which the embryo is protected by several membranes is called a(an) ________________ egg.

18. Birds require an enormous amount of ________________ for flight and for maintaining a constant body temperature.

19. Birds have a(an) ________________ - chambered heart.

20. On a dark, moonless night with overcast skies, some migrating birds may still find their way by following Earth's ________________ field.

Short Answer

In complete sentences, write the answers to the questions on the lines provided.

21. What disadvantage for reptiles does their skin create? How do reptiles overcome this disadvantage?

____

____

22. Compare the lungs of amphibians and reptiles.

____

____

23. Describe a defensive mechanism, other than escape, that reptiles in the order Testudines can use to protect themselves.

____

____

____

____

24. How does structure A in Figure 1 differ from the corresponding structure in other vertebrates?

____

____

____

25. Explain how the shape of the structure labeled B in Figure 1 is an adaptation for flight.

____

____

____

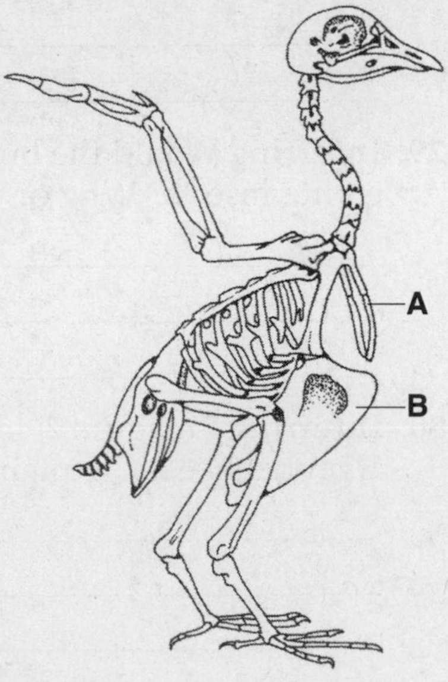

Figure 1

Using Science Skills

Use the diagram below to answer the following questions on the lines provided.

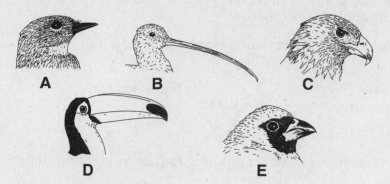

Figure 2

26. **Applying Concepts** Identify the type of food that the bird labeled A in Figure 2 probably eats. Explain your answer.

_____

_____

_____

27. **Inferring** How is the bird labeled B in Figure 2 adapted to feeding in a shallow, wet environment?

_____

_____

_____

28. **Applying Concepts** In Figure 2, identify the type of food that the bird labeled C probably eats. Explain your answer.

_____

_____

_____

29. **Inferring** Would the bird labeled D in Figure 2 be successful at eating insects? Why or why not?

_____

_____

_____

30. **Inferring** In Figure 2, identify the type of food that the bird labeled E probably eats. Explain your answer.

_____

_____

_____

_____

Essay

Write the answer to each question in the space provided.

31. Describe the range of characteristics exhibited by dinosaurs.

32. Compare and contrast the circulatory systems of a lizard and an alligator.

33. Describe the evidence relating to whether *Archaeopteryx* should be classified as a dinosaur or a bird.

34. Describe the flow of air through the respiratory system of a bird. Explain why this pattern of airflow is an advantage for birds.

35. Describe three ways in which birds interact with natural ecosystems and human society.

Chapter 31 Reptiles and Birds   **Chapter Test B**

Multiple Choice

Write the letter that best answers the question or completes the statement on the line provided.

_____ **1.** The only places on Earth where most reptiles cannot live are very
   a. hot areas.
   b. cold areas.
   c. dry areas.

_____ **2.** One way an ectotherm can warm its body is to
   a. move into the shade.
   b. bask in the sun.
   c. speed up its metabolism.

_____ **3.** The earliest known reptiles lived during the
   a. Permian Period.
   b. Triassic Period.
   c. Carboniferous Period.

_____ **4.** Which of the following is NOT thought to have contributed to the extinction of the dinosaurs?
   a. massive volcanic eruptions
   b. the collision of an asteroid or a comet
   c. the rising of sea level

_____ **5.** Most reptiles exchange gases through their
   a. gills.
   b. skin.
   c. lungs.

_____ **6.** The difference between reptilian eggs and amphibian eggs is that reptilian eggs
   a. must develop in water.
   b. always hatch inside the mother's body.
   c. are surrounded by a protective shell and membranes.

_____ **7.** The tuatara belongs to the order
   a. Rhynchocephalia.
   b. Crocodilia.
   c. Testudines.

_____ **8.** Most lizards have all of the following EXCEPT
   a. clawed toes.
   b. a third eye.
   c. movable eyelids.

Name________________________________ Class____________________ Date ______________

____ 9. The dorsal part of a turtle's shell is called the
a. carapace.
b. plastron.
c. amnion.

____10. Which of the following statements is incorrect?
a. All birds can fly.
b. All birds maintain a constant internal body temperature.
c. All birds have two legs.

____11. An endotherm is an animal that
a. has a low rate of metabolism.
b. can generate its own body heat.
c. stores large amounts of food in its stomach.

____12. In which part of a bird's digestive system is food stored and moistened before it enters the stomach?
a. cloaca
b. small intestine
c. crop

____13. One characteristic that *Archaeopteryx* had but most dinosaurs lacked was
a. feathers.
b. teeth.
c. a tail.

____14. The largest order of birds consists of
a. birds of prey.
b. flightless birds.
c. perching birds.

____15. Insect-eating birds are beneficial to human society because they
a. pollinate flowers.
b. help keep mosquito populations under control.
c. disperse seeds.

Completion

Complete each statement on the line provided.

16. In reptiles that live entirely on land, excess water is absorbed from urine in the ____________________.

17. The ____________________ is the ventral part of a turtle's shell.

18. The structure labeled A in Figure 1 is the ____________________.

19. The structure labeled B in Figure 1 is the ____________________.

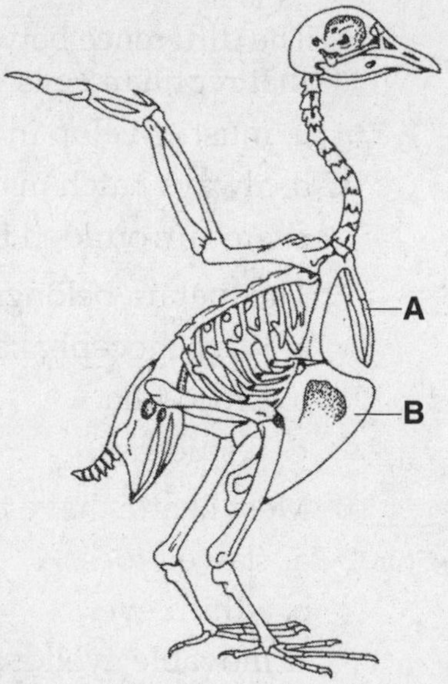

Figure 1

20. The droppings of fruit-eating birds disperse

_____ over great distances.

Short Answer

In complete sentences, write the answers to the questions on the lines provided.

21. Why is it better for a reptile that lives entirely on land to excrete nitrogenous wastes as uric acid instead of ammonia?

_____

_____

_____

_____

_____

22. Describe one threat to the survival of modern reptiles.

_____

_____

_____

_____

23. How do birds heat their bodies?

_____

_____

_____

_____

_____

24. State the two alternative explanations for the evolutionary relationship between birds and dinosaurs.

_____

_____

_____

_____

_____

25. What are two common characteristics of birds of prey?

_____

_____

_____

_____

_____

Name_____ Class_____ Date _____

Using Science Skills

Use the diagram below to answer the following questions on the lines provided.

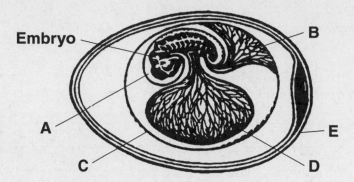

Figure 2

26. **Interpreting Graphics** In Figure 2, identify the structure labeled A, and describe its function.

_____

_____

_____

27. **Interpreting Graphics** Identify the structure labeled B in Figure 2, and describe its function.

_____

_____

_____

28. **Interpreting Graphics** In Figure 2, what are the name and the function of the structure labeled C?

_____

_____

_____

29. **Interpreting Graphics** In Figure 2, what are the name and the function of the structure labeled D?

_____

_____

_____

30. **Applying Concepts** Identify the structure labeled E in Figure 2, and describe its physical characteristics in most reptile eggs.

_____

_____

_____

LESSON PLAN 32–1 (pages 821–827)

Introduction to the Mammals

Time
**2 periods
1 block**

Section Objectives

- **32.1.1 List** the characteristics of mammals.
- **32.1.2 Tell** when mammals evolved.
- **32.1.3 Describe** how mammals perform essential life functions.

Vocabulary mammary gland • subcutaneous fat • rumen • diaphragm • cerebral cortex

Local Standards

1 FOCUS

Vocabulary Preview
Students infer the location of subcutaneous fat based on the derivation of the word *subcutaneous*.

Targeted Resources
❏ Transparencies: **473** Section 32–1 Interest Grabber
❏ Transparencies: **474** Section 32–1 Outline

2 INSTRUCT

Build Science Skills: Posing Questions
Students pose questions paleontologists might ask to identify fossils as mammalian. **L2**

Build Science Skills: Inferring
Students infer various animals' habitats based on the type of hairs in their coats. **L1 L2**

Use Visuals: Figure 32–4
Students compare and contrast herbivore and carnivore teeth. **L1 L2**

Build Science Skills: Inferring
Students infer the amounts of rods and cones in the eyes of nocturnal and diurnal mammals. **L2 L3**

Build Science Skills: Classifying
Students divide different mammalian skeletons into groups based on types of movement. **L2**

Targeted Resources
❏ Reading and Study Workbook: Section 32–1
❏ Adapted Reading and Study Workbook: Section 32–1
❏ Teaching Resources: Section Summaries 32–1, Worksheets 32–1
❏ Transparencies: **475** Structure of a Bear's Heart, **476** Figure 32–4 The Jaws and Teeth of Mammals
❏ BioDetectives DVD: "Wrongly Accused: Science and Justice"
❏ Investigations in Forensics: Investigation 9
❏ Lab Worksheets: Chapter 32 Real-World Lab
❏  **NSTA** *sci*LINKS Mammals

3 ASSESS

Evaluate Understanding
Students match the mammalian characteristics to the mammalian life functions.

Reteach
Student pairs list mammalian characteristics based on observations of the pictures in this section.

Targeted Resources
Teaching Resources: Section Review 32–1
❏ *i*Text Section 32–1

LESSON PLAN 32–2 (pages 828–832)

Diversity of Mammals

Time
1 period
1/2 block

Section Objectives

Local Standards

- **32.2.1 Explain** how the three groups of living mammals differ from one another.
- **32.2.2 Name** the major orders of placental mammals.
- **32.2.3 Describe** how convergent evolution caused mammals on different continents to be similar in form and function.

Vocabulary monotreme • marsupial • placenta

1 FOCUS

Reading Strategy
Students write questions for each subsection and answer them as they read the section.

Targeted Resources
❑ Transparencies: **477** Section 32–2 Interest Grabber
❑ Transparencies: **478** Section 32–2 Outline
❑ Transparencies: **479** Compare/Contrast Table

2 INSTRUCT

Build Science Skills: Comparing and Contrasting
Students make a Venn diagram to compare monotremes and reptiles. **L1** **L2**

Make Connections: Environmental Science
Discuss how the introduction of placental mammals in Australia and New Guinea has affected the native marsupials. **L2** **L3**

Use Visuals: Figure 32–12
Use Figure 32–12 to reinforce the characteristics of the major orders of placental mammals. **L1** **L2**

Build Science Skills: Classifying
Students classify pictures of mammals into orders. **L1** **L2**

Use Visuals: Figure 32–13
Use Figure 32–13 to discuss the concept of convergent evolution. **L2**

Targeted Resources
❑ Reading and Study Workbook: Section 32–2
❑ Adapted Reading and Study Workbook: Section 32–2
❑ Teaching Resources: Section Summaries 32–2, Worksheets 32–2
❑ Transparencies: **480** Figure 32–13 Convergent Evolution of Insect-Eating Mammals

3 ASSESS

Evaluate Understanding
Orally quiz students about the differences among the three groups of mammals.

Reteach
Students construct a table summarizing the orders of placental mammals.

Targeted Resources
Teaching Resources: Section Review 32–2

❑ Section 32–2

LESSON PLAN 32–3 (pages 833–841)

Time
2 periods
1 block

Primates and Human Origins

Section Objectives

- **32.3.1 Identify** the characteristics that all primates share.
- **32.3.2 Describe** the major evolutionary groups of primates.
- **32.3.3 Explain** the current scientific thinking about hominid evolution.

Vocabulary binocular vision • prosimian • anthropoid • prehensile • hominoid • hominid • bipedal • opposable thumb

Local Standards

---

1 FOCUS

Vocabulary Preview
Help students differentiate between *hominoid* and *hominid*.

Targeted Resources
❑ Transparencies: **481** Section 32–3 Interest Grabber
❑ Transparencies: **482** Section 32–3 Outline

---

2 INSTRUCT

Build Science Skills: Applying Concepts
Students explore the importance of flexible digits. **L2**

Build Science Skills: Classifying
Students classify pictures of primates as prosimians or anthropoids. **L2**

Make Connections: Earth Science
Discuss how the New World monkeys and the Old World monkeys evolved differently. **L2**

Address Misconceptions
Dispel the misconception that humans evolved directly from modern apes. **L1 L2**

Build Science Skills: Using Models
Students construct a time line showing when various hominid species lived. **L1 L2**

Use Visuals: Figure 32–18
Use Figure 32–18 to compare and contrast the skulls of hominid fossils. **L2**

Targeted Resources
❑ Reading and Study Workbook: Section 32–3
❑ Adapted Reading and Study Workbook: Section 32–3
❑ Transparencies: **483** Comparison of Skulls of Human Ancestors, **484** Figure 32–16 Human and Gorilla Skeletons
❑ Teaching Resources: Section Summaries 32–3, Worksheets 32–3, Enrichment
❑ BioDetectives DVD: "Mummies: Ties to the Past"
❑ Lab Manual A: Chapter 32 Lab
❑ Lab Manual B: Chapter 32 Lab
❑ **NSTA** *sci*LINKS Human evolution

---

3 ASSESS

Evaluate Understanding
Students make a family tree to show how the primate groups evolved from a common ancestor.

Reteach
Students write definitions for the Vocabulary words in their own words.

Targeted Resources
❑ Teaching Resources: Section Review 32–3, Chapter Vocabulary Review, Graphic Organizer, Chapter 32 Tests: Levels A and B
❑ 〈**iText**〉 Section 32–3, Chapter 32 Assessment
❑ **PHSchool.com** Online Chapter 32 Test

Chapter 32   Mammals

Summary

32–1 Introduction to Mammals

Mammals are animals with hair and mammary glands. In females, mammary glands produce milk to nourish the young. **All mammals breathe air, have four-chambered hearts, and are endotherms that generate their body heat internally.**

Mammals descended from ancient reptiles. **The first true mammals appeared during the late Triassic Period, about 220 million years ago.** These mammals were small and active only at night. When dinosaurs became extinct, mammals evolved to fill many niches.

Mammals have many adaptations that make them suitable to a wide range of habitats.

- Body Temperature Control. Mammals are endotherms. Their metabolism creates their body heat. Mammals have a layer of **subcutaneous fat** and fur or hair to prevent heat loss. Many mammals release heat through sweat glands. The ability of mammals to regulate their body heat from within is an example of homeostasis.
- Feeding. Mammals eat a great deal of food to maintain their high metabolic rate. Early mammals ate insects. **As mammals evolved, the form and function of their jaws and teeth became adapted to eat foods other than insects.** Mammals have specialized teeth, jaws, and digestive systems for eating plants, animals, or both.
- Respiration. All mammals breathe with lungs. Mammals share well-developed chest muscles, including a **diaphragm,** that separates the chest cavity from the abdomen. The diaphragm, along with other muscles in the chest, help pull air into the lungs and push air out.
- Circulation. Mammals have a double-loop circulatory system. They also have a four-chambered heart. Each side of the heart has an atrium and a ventricle. This arrangement separates oxygen-rich blood from oxygen-poor blood.
- Excretion. The kidneys of mammals are highly developed. This lets mammals live in many habitats. **The kidneys of mammals help maintain homeostasis by filtering urea from the blood, as well as by excreting excess water or retaining needed water.**

- <u>Response</u>. Mammals have the most highly developed brain of any animal. Mammalian brains have a cerebrum, cerebellum, and medulla oblongata. The cerebrum has a well-developed outer layer called the **cerebral cortex.** It is the center of thinking and other complex behaviors. The cerebellum coordinates movements. The medulla oblongata regulates involuntary body functions such as breathing and heart rate.
- <u>Movement</u>. Mammals have adapted to living on land, in water, and in the air. Variations in limb bone structure allow mammals to run, walk, climb, burrow, hop, fly, and swim.
- <u>Reproduction</u>. Mammals have adaptations that help them reproduce successfully. All mammals reproduce by internal fertilization. Newborn mammals feed on milk from the mother. Most mammal parents care for their young after birth. The length of care varies among species.

32–2 Diversity of Mammals

Mammals are divided into three groups: monotremes, marsupials, and placentals. The three groups of mammals differ in their means of reproduction and development.

- **Monotremes lay eggs.** They also have a cloaca, similar to that of reptiles. When the soft-shelled eggs hatch, the young are nourished by their mother's milk. The duckbill platypus is an example of a monotreme.
- **Marsupials bear live young. The young are born at an early stage of development.** Soon after birth, the young crawl across the mother's fur and attach to a nipple inside the mother's pouch. The young continue nursing until they are able to live on their own. Marsupials include kangaroos and koalas.
- Most mammals are **placental mammals. In placental mammals, nutrients, oxygen, carbon dioxide, and wastes are exchanged efficiently between embryo and mother through the placenta.** After the birth of young, most placental mammals care for their offspring. Dogs, whales, and humans are examples of placental mammals.

There are twelve main orders of placental mammals. Two of these orders are adapted to life in the water. Sirenians are herbivores that live fully aquatic lives. Cetaceans are aquatic mammals that must come to the surface of the water to breathe. Chiropterans are the winged mammals, or bats. The land-based placental mammals include insectivores, rodents, perissodactyls, carnivores, artiodactyls, lagomorphs, xenarthrans, primates, and proboscideans.

32–3 Primates and Human Origins

All primates share several key adaptations. They have binocular vision, a well-developed cerebrum, relatively long fingers and toes, and arms that rotate in broad circles around the shoulder joints.

Early in their evolutionary history, primates split into several groups. **Primates that evolved from two of the earliest branches look very little like typical monkeys and are called prosimians.** These animals are small, nocturnal primates. They have large eyes adapted for seeing in the dark.

Members of the more familiar primate group that includes monkeys, apes, and humans are called anthropoids. The anthropoids split into two major groups.

- New World monkeys. These monkeys now live in Central and South America. All New World monkeys have a **prehensile tail.** These tails can coil tightly enough around a branch to serve as a "fifth hand."
- Old World monkeys and the great apes. Old World monkeys do not have prehensile tails. Great apes are also called **hominoids.** This group includes gorillas, chimpanzees, and humans. The hominoid line gave rise to the branch that leads to modern humans. This group, called the **hominids,** evolved adaptations for upright walking. They have thumbs adapted for grasping as well as larger brains.

Recent fossil finds have changed the way paleontologists think about hominid evolution. **Researchers now believe that hominid evolution occurred in a series of adaptive radiations. This process led to several different species instead of one species that led directly to the next.**

Our genus, *Homo,* first appeared in Africa. Researchers do not agree when the first hominids began migrating from Africa. They are also unsure about when and where *Homo sapiens* arose. The multi-regional model suggests that modern humans evolved independently in several parts of the world. The out-of-Africa model proposes that modern humans arose in Africa and then migrated away.

About 100,000 years ago, two main groups of hominids existed: *Homo neanderthalensis* and *Homo sapiens.* Fossil evidence suggests that these hominids used stone tools and lived in similar ways.

About 50,000–40,000 years ago, *Homo sapiens* changed their way of life. These hominids made more sophisticated tools. They drew cave paintings. They also began burying their dead with elaborate rituals. In these ways, they began acting more like modern humans. The Neanderthals disappeared about 30,000 years ago. Since then, *Homo sapiens* has been the only hominid on Earth.

Mammalian Teeth

Mammals have three kinds of teeth. Canines are pointed teeth that pierce, grip, and tear. Incisors are chisel-like teeth that cut and gnaw. Molars and premolars crush and grind food.

Color the incisors blue. Color the molars and premolars yellow. The canines have been shaded for you.

Carnivore

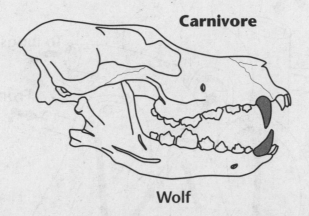

Wolf

Herbivore

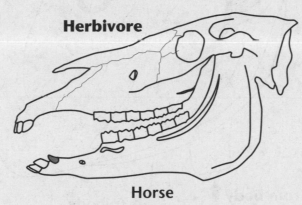

Horse

Use the diagrams to answer the questions.

1. Which animal has larger canines? Circle the correct answer.

   wolf   horse

2. Think about your answer to question 1. Why does the animal you chose need larger canines?

   _____

   _____

3. For what purpose does a horse use its premolars and molars?

   _____

Mammalian Heart

Color the parts of the heart that hold oxygen-rich blood red. Color the parts of the heart that hold oxygen-poor blood blue.

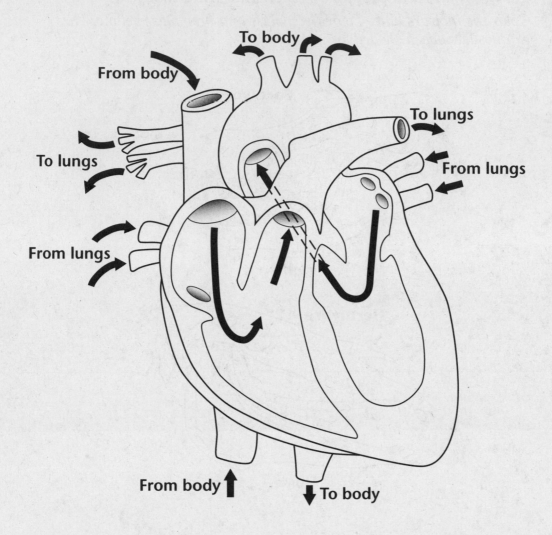

Use the diagram to answer the questions.

1. Oxygen-poor blood flows from the heart to the

   _____.

2. Oxygen-rich blood flows from the lungs to the

   _____.

3. Oxygen-rich blood flows from the heart to the

   _____.

Mammal Limbs, Fingers, and Toes

Homologous structures are those that develop from the same embryonic tissue in different organisms. The structures may look different when the organisms are mature. Look at the picture of monkey and horse bones. The bones labeled with the same color are homologous.

Color the monkey and horse bones as marked. Then color the homologous bones in the other three animals the same colors. (Hint: You may want to look at pages 826–827 in your textbook for help.)

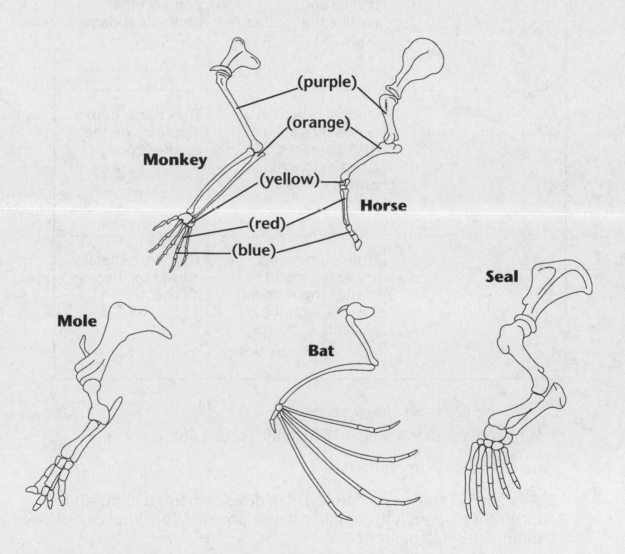

Use the diagrams to answer the question.

1. Which animal has adapted to fly?

_____

Diversity of Mammals

There are three groups of living mammals: monotremes, marsupials, and placental mammals.

Write the name of each group in the correct place in the table.

Group	How Are Young Born?	How Are Young Fed?
	They hatch from soft-shelled eggs laid outside the mother's body.	They lick milk from pores on the mother's abdomen.
	Embryo is born at a very early stage of development and attaches to a nipple, usually inside a pouch.	They nurse from a nipple inside the mother's pouch.
	Embryos develop inside the mother. Wastes and nutrients pass through the placenta.	They are generally nursed by the mother.

Use the table to answer the questions.

1. Which mammals lay eggs? Circle the correct answer.

   marsupials   monotremes

2. A kangaroo embryo is born early in development. It climbs into its mother's pouch to complete development. What kind of mammal is a kangaroo?

   _____

3. Humans, sea lions, cats, dogs, and mice are all examples of what type of mammal? Circle the correct answer.

   placental   monotremes

Primate Evolution

The cladogram shows how scientists believe modern primates are related to one another and to their common primate ancestor. The earliest two branches are called prosimians. The other primates are anthropoids. Anthropoids include New World monkeys, Old World monkeys, and the great apes, or hominoids.

Color the branches for prosimians red. Color the branches for anthropoids blue. Then, circle the hominoids.

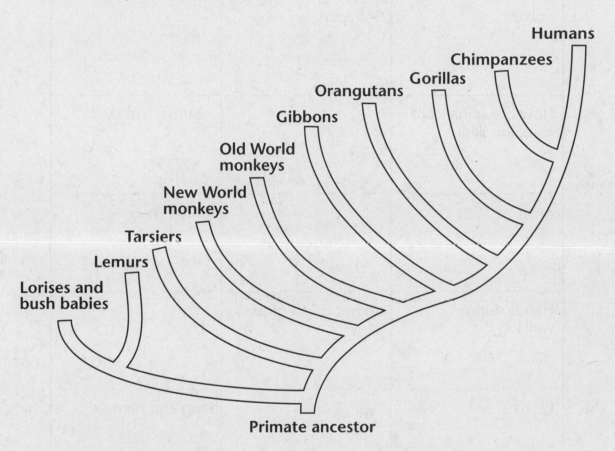

Use the cladogram to answer the questions. Circle the correct answer.

1. Which primate is a prosimian?

    gibbon   lemur

2. Which primate is a hominoid?

    Old World monkey   orangutan

Human and Gorilla Skeletons

The skeleton of a modern human is adapted to walk upright on two legs. Gorillas use all four limbs.

Complete the table. Describe each feature in humans and gorillas. Some items have been completed for you

Feature	Human	Gorilla
Spine	S-shaped	
How the spinal cord exits the skull		near back of skull
Arms		longer than legs
Hands during walking	do not touch ground	
Pelvis		long and narrow
Angle of thigh bones	inward	

Use the table to answer the question.

1. Describe the spine of a gorilla.

_____

Early Hominids

The timeline shows some fossil hominids that scientists have discovered. The bar shows the time ranges during which each species may have existed. Each species has a genus name and a species name.

Color the bars for all the species in the genus Homo *red. Color the bars for all the species in the genus* Australopithecus *blue. Color the bars for all the species in the genus* Paranthropus *yellow.*

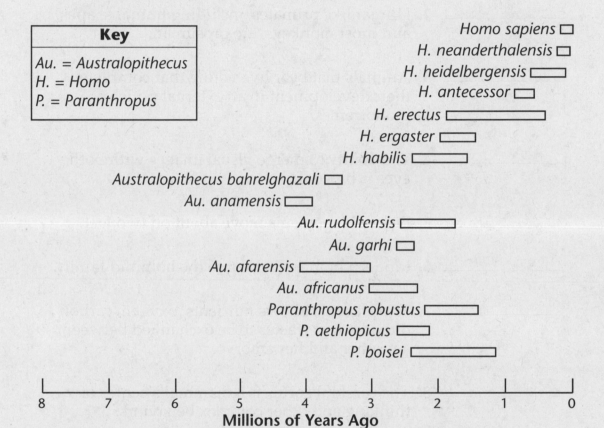

Key
Au. = Australopithecus
H. = Homo
P. = Paranthropus

Homo sapiens
H. neanderthalensis
H. heidelbergensis
H. antecessor
H. erectus
H. ergaster
H. habilis
Australopithecus bahrelghazali
Au. anamensis
Au. rudolfensis
Au. garhi
Au. afarensis
Au. africanus
Paranthropus robustus
P. aethiopicus
P. boisei

8   7   6   5   4   3   2   1   0

Millions of Years Ago

Use the timeline to answer the questions. Circle the correct answer.

1. Which hominid probably existed earlier?

   Australopithecus africanus   *Homo neanderthalensis*

2. Is hominid evolution a simple straight-line transformation from one species to another? Explain.

   _____

   _____

Chapter 32   Mammals

Vocabulary Review

True or False   *If the statement is true, write* true. *If it is false, write* false.

_____ 1. An opposable thumb enables hominids to grasp objects.

_____ 2. Humanlike primates, including humans, apes, and most monkeys, are prosimians.

_____ 3. Animals that bear live young that complete their development in an external pouch are monotremes.

_____ 4. The ability to merge visual images with both eyes is bipedal.

_____ 5. Bipedal organisms move about on two feet.

_____ 6. Modern humans belong to the hominid family.

_____ 7. The placenta allows nutrients, oxygen, carbon dioxide, and wastes to be exchanged between a mother and her embryo.

_____ 8. The cerebral cortex is a mammal's center of thinking and other complex behaviors.

_____ 9. The diaphragm is a powerful muscle at the base of the chest cavity that is used for breathing.

_____ 10. The great apes are also called prosimians.

Summary

32–1 Introduction to the Mammals

All mammals have hair and mammary glands. In females, mammary glands produce milk to nourish the young. In addition to hair and mammary glands, all mammals breathe air, have four-chambered hearts, and can generate their body heat internally.

Mammals descended from ancient reptiles. Early mammals, which lived during the time of dinosaurs, were small and active only at night. When the dinosaurs became extinct, mammals evolved to fill many different niches.

Mammals have many different adaptations that allow them to live in diverse habitats. Like birds, mammals are endotherms. Their metabolism creates their body heat. They have body fat and fur or hair to prevent heat loss. Many have sweat glands to conserve body heat.

Mammals must eat a lot of food to maintain their high metabolic rate. Mammals have specialized teeth, jaws, and digestive systems for eating plants or animals or both.

All mammals use lungs to breathe. Well-developed muscles in the chest, including the diaphragm, help pull air into the lungs and push air out.

Mammals have a four-chambered heart and a double-loop circulatory system. One loop brings blood to and from the lungs, and the other loop brings blood to and from the rest of the body. Each side of the heart has an atrium and a ventricle. Oxygen-rich blood is completely separated from oxygen-poor blood.

Highly developed kidneys help control the amount of water in the body. This enables mammals to live in many different habitats. The kidneys filter nitrogenous wastes from the blood, forming urine.

Mammals have the most highly developed brains of any animals. Mammalian brains consist of a cerebrum, cerebellum, and medulla oblongata. The cerebrum contains a well-developed outer layer called the cerebral cortex. It is the center of thinking and other complex behaviors.

Mammals, like other vertebrates, have endocrine glands that are part of an endocrine system. Endocrine glands regulate body activities by releasing hormones that affect other organs and tissues.

Mammals have many different adaptations for movement. Variations in the structure of limb bones allow mammals to run, walk, climb, burrow, hop, fly, and swim.

Mammals reproduce by internal fertilization. All newborn mammals feed on the mother's milk. Most mammal parents care for their young for a certain amount of time after birth. The length of care varies among species.

32–2 Diversity of Mammals

The three groups of living mammals are the monotremes, marsupials, and placentals. They differ in their means of reproduction and development. Monotremes lay eggs. They also have a cloaca, similar to the cloaca of reptiles. When the soft-shelled monotreme eggs hatch, the young are nourished by the mother's milk.

Marsupials bear live young that complete their development in an external pouch. The young are born at a very early stage of development. They crawl across the mother's fur and attach to a nipple. They continue to drink milk until they are large enough to survive on their own.

Placental mammals are the most familiar. Placental mammals are named for the placenta—an internal structure that is formed when the embryo's tissues join with tissues from within the mother's body. Nutrients, oxygen, carbon dioxide, and wastes are passed between the embryo and mother through the placenta. After birth, most placental mammals care for their offspring.

32–3 Primates and Human Origins

All primates share several important adaptations. Many of these adaptations are useful for a life spent mainly in trees. These adaptations include binocular vision, a well-developed cerebrum, flexible fingers and toes, and arms that rotate in broad circles.

Very early in evolutionary history, primates split into several groups. Prosimians are small, nocturnal primates with large eyes adapted for seeing in the dark. Anthropoids include monkeys, apes, and humans.

Very early in their evolutionary history, anthropoids split into two major groups. One group evolved into the monkeys found today in Central and South America. This group is called the New World monkeys. All New World monkeys have a prehensile tale. A prehensile tail is a tail that can coil tightly around a branch to serve as a "fifth hand." The other group of anthropoids includes the Old World monkeys and the great apes. Old World monkeys do not have prehensile tails. Great apes, which are also called hominoids, include gorillas, chimpanzees, and humans.

The hominoid line gave rise to the branch that leads to modern humans. This group, called the hominids, evolved adaptations for upright walking, thumbs adapted for grasping, and larger brains.

Many recent fossil finds have changed the way paleontologists think about hominid evolution. Now researchers think that hominid evolution occurred in a series of complex adaptive radiations. This produced a large number of different species rather than one species that led directly to the next.

Researchers agree that our genus, *Homo*, first appeared in Africa. However, researchers do not agree when the first hominids began migrating from Africa. They are also not sure when and where *Homo sapiens* arose. The multiregional model suggests that modern humans evolved independently in several parts of the world. The out-of-Africa model proposes that modern humans arose in Africa and then migrated out.

About 500,000 years ago, two main groups of hominids are known to have existed. *Homo neanderthalensis* lived in Europe and western Asia. Fossil evidence suggests that they used stone tools and lived in organized groups. The other group is the first *Homo sapiens*. Researchers think that they lived side by side with Neanderthals.

According to one hypothesis, around 50,000–40,000 years ago, *H. sapiens* dramatically changed their way of life. They made more sophisticated tools. They produced cave paintings. They also began burying their dead with elaborate rituals. In other words, they began to behave more like modern humans. The Neanderthals disappeared about 30,000 years ago. It is not yet known why. Since then, *H. sapiens* has been the only hominid on Earth.

Section 32–1 Introduction to the Mammals
(pages 821–827)

🔑 Key Concepts
- What are the characteristics of mammals?
- When did mammals evolve?
- How do mammals maintain homeostasis?

Introduction (page 821)

1. List the two notable features of mammals.

    a. _____

    b. _____

2. Circle the letter of each characteristic of mammals.

    a. breathe air   c. ectotherm

    b. three-chambered heart   d. endotherm

Evolution of Mammals (page 821)

3. What three characteristics help scientists identify mammalian fossils?

    a. _____

    b. _____

    c. _____

4. The ancestors of mammals diverged from ancient _____ during the Permian Period.

5. Circle the letter of each sentence that is true about the evolution of mammals.

    a. The first true mammals were as large as dinosaurs.

    b. During the Cretaceous Period, mammals were probably nocturnal.

    c. After dinosaurs disappeared, mammals increased in size and filled many new niches.

    d. The Permian Period is usually called the Age of Mammals.

Form and Function in Mammals (pages 822–827)

6. List two ways in which mammals conserve body heat.

    a. _____

    b. _____

7. Is the following sentence true or false? Mammals have a low rate of metabolism.
   _____

8. Circle the letter of each way mammals are able to rid themselves of excess heat.
   a. fat   c. sweat glands
   b. hair   d. panting

9. The ability of mammals to regulate their body heat from within is an example of
   _____.

10. Is the following sentence true or false? Animals that are omnivores consume only
    meat. _____

11. As mammals evolved, the form and function of their _____ and
    _____ became adapted to eat foods other than insects.

12. Complete the table about the different kinds of teeth found in mammals.

TEETH ADAPTATIONS IN MAMMALS

Type	Description
Canines	
	Chisellike incisors used for cutting, gnawing, and grooming
Molars and premolars	

13. In which type of animal would you expect to find sharp canine teeth? _____

14. How are herbivores' molars adapted for their diet? _____
    _____
    _____

15. Is the following sentence true or false? Carnivores have a shorter intestine than
    herbivores. _____

16. Complete the flowchart to show how cows digest their food.

Newly swallowed food is stored and processed in the _____.

↓

Symbiotic bacteria in the rumen digest the _____ of most plant tissues.

↓

The cow _____ the food from the rumen into its mouth, and food is chewed and swallowed again.

↓

The food is swallowed again and moves through the rest of the _____ and _____.

17. How does the diaphragm work to help move air into and out of the lungs?

_____

_____

_____

_____

18. Is the following sentence true or false? Mammals have a four-chambered heart that pumps blood into two separate circuits around the body. _____

19. Where does the right side of the heart pump oxygen-poor blood? _____

20. After blood picks up oxygen in the lungs, where does it go? _____

_____

21. How do mammalian kidneys help to maintain homeostasis? _____

_____

_____

_____

Match each part of the mammalian brain with its function.

Part of the brain	Function
_____ **22.** medulla oblongata	**a.** Involved in thinking and learning
_____ **23.** cerebral cortex	**b.** Controls muscular coordination
_____ **24.** cerebrum	**c.** Regulates involuntary body functions
_____ **25.** cerebellum	**d.** Part of the cerebrum that is the center of thinking and other complex behaviors

26. What are endocrine glands? _____

_____

_____

27. What body system helps to protect mammals from disease? _____

28. Is the following sentence true or false? Mammals have a rigid backbone, as well as rigid shoulder and pelvic girdles for extra stability. _____

29. Mammals reproduce by _____ fertilization.

30. Is the following sentence true or false? All mammals are viviparous, or live-bearing.

_____

31. What do young mammals learn from their parents? _____

_____

_____

Section 32–2 Diversity of Mammals (pages 828–832)

⊂⊃ **Key Concepts**
- How do the three groups of living mammals differ from one another?
- How did convergent evolution cause mammals on different continents to be similar in form and function?

Introduction (page 828)

1. List the three groups of living mammals.

    a. _____   b. _____   c. _____

2. The three groups of mammals differ greatly in their means of _____ and development.

Monotremes and Marsupials (pages 828–829)

3. The mammals that lay eggs are _____. Those that bear live

    young at a very early stage of development are _____.

4. What two characteristics do monotremes share with reptiles?

    a. _____

    _____

    b. _____

    _____

5. How do monotremes differ from reptiles? _____

    _____

6. Circle the letter of each mammal that is a marsupial.

    a. koala   **c.** platypus

    b. echidna   **d.** kangaroo

7. Describe how marsupial embryos develop. _____

    _____

    _____

    _____

    _____

Placental Mammals (pages 829–831)

8. What is the placenta? _____

    _____

    _____

9. What four substances are exchanged between the embryo and the mother through the placenta?

a. _____   c. _____

b. _____   d. _____

10. Is the following sentence true or false? After birth, most placental mammals care for their young and provide them with nourishment by nursing. _____

Match the main order of placental mammal with its description. Use Figure 32–12 on pages 830–831.

Order

_____ **11.** Insectivores

_____ **12.** Sirenians

_____ **13.** Chiropterans

_____ **14.** Artiodactyls

_____ **15.** Proboscideans

_____ **16.** Lagomorphs

Description

a. Hoofed mammals with an even number of digits on each foot

b. Herbivores with two pairs of incisors in the upper jaw and hind legs adapted for leaping

c. Herbivores that live in rivers, bays, and warm coastal waters

d. The only mammals capable of true flight

e. Insect eaters with long, narrow snouts and sharp claws

f. Mammals that have trunks

Biogeography of Mammals (page 832)

17. Is the following sentence true or false? During the Paleozoic Era, the continents were one large landmass. _____

18. What effect on the evolution of mammals was caused when the continents drifted apart? _____

_____

_____

_____

_____

Reading Skill Practice

A compare-and-contrast table is a useful tool for organizing similarities and differences. Make a table to compare the three groups of living mammals. Include information about the reproduction and development of each group. For more information about compare-and-contrast tables, look in Appendix A of your textbook. Do your work on a separate sheet of paper.

Section 32–3 Primates and Human Origins
(pages 833–841)

👁 Key Concepts
- What characteristics do all primates share?
- What are the major evolutionary groups of primates?
- What is the current scientific thinking about hominid evolution?

What Is a Primate? (pages 833–834)

1. What characteristic distinguished the first primates from other mammals? _____
_____
_____

2. List four adaptations that are shared by primates.

   a. _____

   b. _____

   c. _____

   d. _____

3. Circle the letter of each sentence that is true about primates.

   a. Primates are well adapted to a life of running on the ground.

   b. Many primates can hold objects firmly in their hands.

   c. A well-developed cerebrum enables primates to display elaborate social behaviors.

   d. Because primates have a flat face, both eyes point to the sides.

4. What is binocular vision? _____
_____
_____
_____

Evolution of Primates (pages 834–835)

5. Circle the letter of each characteristic of prosimians.

   a. nocturnal   b. diurnal   c. small in size   d. small eyes

Match the characteristics to the anthropoid group. Each anthropoid group may be used more than once.

Characteristic	Anthropoid Group
_____ 6. Found today in Central and South America	a. New World monkeys
_____ 7. Found today in Africa and Asia	b. Old World monkeys
_____ 8. Includes baboons and macaques	
_____ 9. Includes squirrel monkeys and spider monkeys	
_____ 10. Lack prehensile tails	
_____ 11. Long, prehensile tails and long, flexible arms	

12. Complete the concept map to show the evolution of primates.

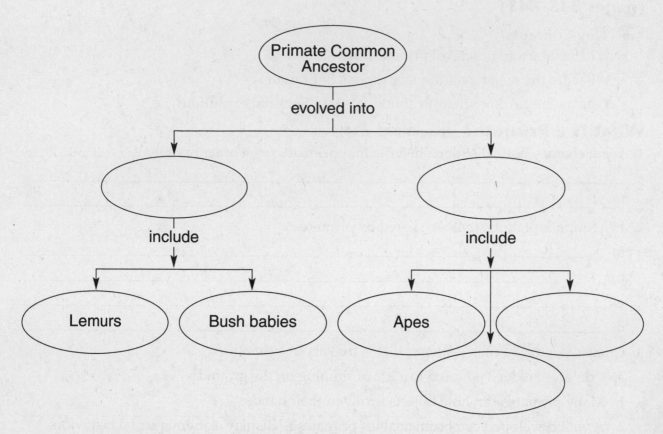

13. The anthropoid group that includes Old World monkeys also includes the great apes, or _____.

Hominid Evolution (pages 835–838)

14. What was the importance of bipedal locomotion that evolved in the hominid family?

_____

_____

15. The hominid hand evolved a(an) _____ thumb that enabled grasping objects and using tools.

16. Is the following sentence true or false? Hominids have a much larger brain than the other hominoids, such as chimpanzees. _____

17. Is the following sentence true or false? Only one fossil species exists that links humans with their nonhuman primate ancestors. _____

18. Circle the letter of each characteristic of the hominid genus *Australopithecus*.

a. bipedal apes

b. never lived in trees

c. fruit eaters

d. very large brains

19. Is the following sentence true or false? Fossil evidence shows that hominids walked bipedally long before they had large brains. _____

20. Based on their teeth, what kind of diet did the known *Paranthropus* species probably eat? _____

21. Is the following sentence true or false? Currently, researchers completely understand the evolution of the hominid species. _____

The Road to Modern Humans (pages 839–840)

22. *Homo habilis* was found with tools made of _____.

23. Describe the two hypotheses that explain how modern *Homo sapiens* might have evolved from earlier members of the genus *Homo*.

a. _____

_____

b. _____

_____

Modern *Homo sapiens* (page 841)

24. Circle the letter of each characteristic of Neanderthals.

a. stone tools

b. lived in social groups

c. gave rise to *H. sapiens*

d. made cave paintings

25. Is the following sentence true or false? Neanderthals and *Homo sapiens* lived side by side for around 50,000 years. _____

26. What fundamental changes did some populations of *H. sapiens* make to their way of life around 50,000–40,000 years ago? _____

_____

Vocabulary Review

Multiple Choice   *In the space provided, write the letter of the answer that best completes each sentence.*

_____ **1.** Mammals are characterized by hair and
   a. lungs.
   b. mammary glands.
   c. four-chambered hearts.
   d. prehensile tails.

_____ **2.** The outer layer of the cerebrum that is the center of thinking is the
   a. cerebellum.
   b. medulla oblongata.
   c. cerebral cortex.
   d. subcutaneous fat.

_____ **3.** Mammals that lay eggs are
   a. monotremes.
   b. placental mammals.
   c. marsupials.
   d. primates.

_____ **4.** Small, nocturnal primates with large eyes adapted to seeing in the dark belong to the primate group called
   a. prosimians.
   b. hominoids.
   c. anthropoids.
   d. hominids.

_____ **5.** Members of the primate group in which the only living members are humans are called
   a. prosimians.
   b. hominoids.
   c. anthropoids.
   d. hominids.

Completion   *Fill in the blanks with terms from Chapter 32.*

6. The layer of fat located beneath the skin is called _____.

7. The _____ is a stomach chamber in which newly swallowed plant food is stored and processed.

8. A powerful muscle called the _____ pulls the bottom of the chest cavity downward, pulling air into the lungs.

9. Mammals bearing live young that complete their development in a pouch are called _____.

10. A structure called a(an) _____ forms when an embryo's tissues join with tissues from the mother's body.

11. The ability to merge visual images from both eyes is called _____.

12. Members of the primate group that includes monkeys, apes, and humans are called _____.

13. A tail that can coil tightly around a branch is called a(an) _____ tail.

14. The evolution of _____, or two-foot, locomotion freed the hands to use tools.

15. The hominid hand evolved a(an) _____ that enabled grasping objects and using tools.

Reviewing Key Concepts

Short Answer *On the lines provided, write* Yes *if the characteristic describes a mammal. Write* No *if it does not.*

1. _____ has hair

2. _____ has a three-chambered heart

3. _____ breathes air

4. _____ is an ectotherm

5. _____ feeds young with milk

Short Answer *On the lines provided, answer the following questions.*

6. When did the first true mammals appear?

_____

_____

_____

7. With respect to feeding, how did the evolution of jaws and teeth help the mammal?

_____

_____

_____

8. How do kidneys help maintain homeostasis in mammals?

_____

_____

_____

Reviewing Key Skills

9. **Inferring** To use the energy in the foods that they eat, animals need oxygen. Would you expect a mammal to need more or less oxygen than a reptile of the same size? Explain your answer.

_____

_____

_____

10. **Comparing and Contrasting** How do the teeth of herbivores and carnivores differ?

_____

_____

_____

Chapter 32 Mammals   **Section Review 32-2**

Reviewing Key Concepts

Identification *On the lines provided, write the group or groups of mammals that are described.*

          monotremes   marsupials   placentals

1. egg-laying mammals _____

2. young develop for a long time before birth _____

3. include kangaroos and koalas _____

4. complete development in an external pouch _____

5. nutrients, gases, and wastes exchanged between embryo and mother

   through a placenta _____

6. share some reproductive characteristics with reptiles _____

7. have a cloaca _____

Short Answer *On the lines provided, answer the following questions.*

8. How do young monotremes obtain milk from their mothers?

   _____

9. Describe the function of a marsupium.

   _____

10. Describe the function of a placenta.

   _____

11. What geological event, early in the Cenozoic Era, set the stage for the convergent evolution of mammals?

   _____

Reviewing Key Skills

Classifying *On the lines provided, classify the following mammals as a* placental, monotreme, *or* marsupial.

12. _____   13. _____

14. _____   15. _____

Reviewing Key Concepts

Completion *On the lines provided, complete the following sentences.*

1. Primates have the ability to merge visual images from both eyes, which is called
   _____ .

2. Primates display complex behaviors because the part of their brain
   called the _____ is well developed.

3. All primates have arms that can rotate in broad circles around their
   _____ joints.

4. The _____ and _____ of
   primates are flexible, enabling them to grasp objects and run along
   tree limbs.

5. The two major evolutionary groups of primates are
   _____ and _____.

6. Most paleontologists think that hominid evolution occurred as a
   series of complex _____ that produced a large
   number of species.

Reviewing Key Skills

7. **Comparing and Contrasting** Compare Old World monkeys and
   New World monkeys.

   _____

   _____

8. **Applying Concepts** Why were the evolution of bipedal locomotion
   and opposable thumbs important developments in the evolution of
   hominids?

   _____

   _____

9. **Inferring** Why do paleontologists frequently revise their ideas about
   the evolutionary relationships of hominid species?

   _____

   _____

10. **Inferring** DNA analyses are used to study human evolution.
    Explain how DNA evidence would support the hypothesis that
    humans evolved from other primates.

    _____

    _____

Chapter 32 Mammals   **Chapter Vocabulary Review**

Matching *On the lines provided, write the letter of the definition that matches each term on the left.*

_____ 1. mammary glands   a. a layer of fat located under the skin

_____ 2. subcutaneous fat   b. small, nocturnal primate with large eyes

_____ 3. rumen   c. center of thinking and complex behavior

_____ 4. diaphragm   d. able to coil tightly around an object

_____ 5. cerebral cortex   e. produce milk to nourish young

_____ 6. binocular vision   f. one stomach chamber of a grazing mammal

_____ 7. prosimian   g. muscle that expands the chest cavity

_____ 8. prehensile   h. ability to merge visual images from both eyes

_____ 9. hominid   i. upright, two-footed motion

_____ 10. bipedal locomotion j. primate that walks upright, has opposable
                                         thumbs, and has a large brain

Completion *On the lines provided, write the word that best completes the sentence.*

11. Egg-laying mammals are called _____.

12. Kangaroos, koalas, and wombats are examples of _____.

13. The structure that allows for the exchange of nutrients, oxygen, carbon dioxide, and wastes between an embryo and mother is called the _____.

14. Members of the primate group that includes monkeys, apes and humans are called _____.

15. A(an) _____ thumb enables humans to grasp objects.

Multiple Choice *On the line provided, write the letter of the answer that best answers the question.*

_____ 16. Which of the following animals does NOT have subcutaneous fat?

a.    c.

b.    d.

_____ **17.** Which of these muscles pulls the bottom of the chest cavity downward?

    a. heart

    b. lungs

    c. kidneys

    d. diaphragm

_____ **18.** Bush babies, lemurs, and tarsiers are

    a. prosimians.

    b. anthropoids.

    c. marsupials.

    d. monotremes.

_____ **19.** Which of the following animals has a prehensile tail?

a.    c.

b.    d.

_____ **20.** Apes are examples of

    a. hominoids.

    b. Old World monkeys.

    c. prosimians.

    d. hominids.

Chapter 32 Mammals   Enrichment

The Research of Jane Goodall and Dian Fossey

Jane Goodall is known as a pioneer in primate behavior studies. She was born in England in 1934. In 1957, she went to Tanzania on a vacation and met Louis Leakey, a paleontologist. Leakey hired Goodall as an assistant secretary, and he suggested that she observe the wild chimpanzees that lived on the shores of Lake Tanganyika. At a time when studies of animal behavior were becoming more quantitative and impersonal, Goodall's accounts of chimpanzees were intuitive personal narratives. She wrote for *National Geographic Magazine* and became a spokesperson for the chimps, showing the parallels between chimp and human life.

Goodall's original studies took her into the camps in which chimps lived. There, at times, she tried to become an active participant in chimp life. Later, she decided that observation, rather than participation, was the best mode of study. Goodall observed tool use among chimps, as well as cannibalism, violence, and infanticide. Her work has led to a worldwide appreciation of the similarities and differences among non-human primates.

Goodall raised her son, Hugo, at the study camp in Gombe. Goodall currently spends much of her time traveling around the world speaking about her experiences and talking with schoolchildren. She has written many books about her studies of chimps.

Dian Fossey followed the path begun by Goodall. She was a behavioral scientist, known for her studies of the rare mountain gorilla in east central Africa. Fossey observed gorillas in their natural habitat, keeping her studies as isolated from the outside world as possible.

Dian Fossey was a dedicated conservationist. She organized and carried out antipoaching raids in Africa in the 1980s. She witnessed abuse of the gorillas with whom she lived and studied, and she saw them tortured and killed by poachers. Dian Fossey fought back by burning the poachers' homes and destroying their possessions. She believed that, to save the gorilla, she needed to take the law into her own hands. Fossey was killed in 1985, and she was buried in the same graveyard she had created for the gorillas she loved.

Evaluation *Answer the following questions on a separate sheet of paper.*

1. Why do you think Jane Goodall decided to use observation rather than participation to learn about the chimpanzees? Are there things she could learn by one method but not by the other? Explain your answer.

2. How was the work of Dian Fossey similar to that of Jane Goodall? How was it different?

Concept Map

Using information from the chapter, complete the concept map below. If there is not enough room in the concept map to write your answers, write them on a separate sheet of paper.

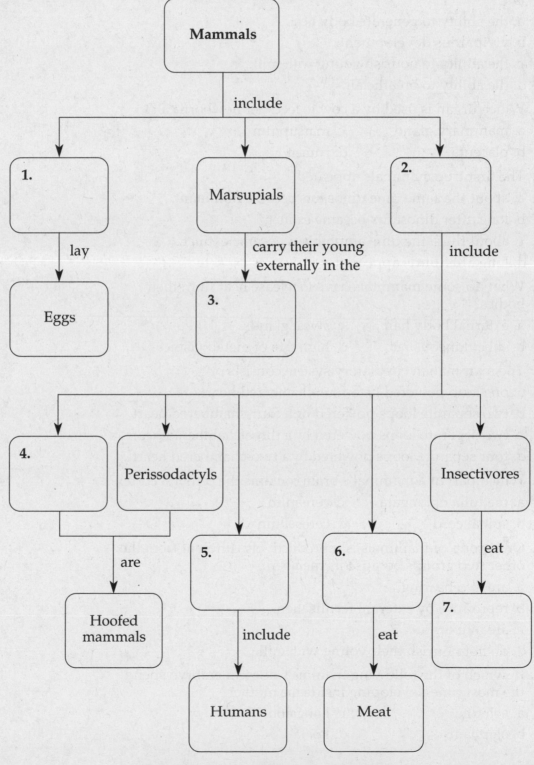

Multiple Choice

Write the letter that best answers the question or completes the statement on the line provided.

_____ **1.** A feature that is present in most but NOT all female mammals is
   a. the ability to generate body heat.
   b. viviparous development.
   c. the ability to nourish young with milk.
   d. the ability to breathe air.

_____ **2.** Which organ is used by a cow to feed her newborn calf?
   a. mammary gland   c. marsupium
   b. placenta   d. rumen

_____ **3.** The first true mammals appeared
   a. about the same time dinosaurs became dominant.
   b. long after dinosaurs became extinct.
   c. about the same time amphibians became extinct.
   d. long after birds appeared.

_____ **4.** What do some mammals have to release heat from their bodies?
   a. external body hair   c. sweat glands
   b. subcutaneous fat   d. high rate of metabolism

_____ **5.** The mammalian circulatory system consists of
   a. one loop powered by a four-chambered heart.
   b. two separate loops powered by a four-chambered heart.
   c. two separate loops powered by a three-chambered heart.
   d. four separate loops powered by a two-chambered heart.

_____ **6.** Which part of a mammal's brain contains the cerebral cortex?
   a. medulla oblongata   c. cerebrum
   b. spinal cord   d. cerebellum

_____ **7.** One group of mammals is reproductively different from the other two groups because its members
   a. are live-bearing.
   b. reproduce by external fertilization.
   c. are oviparous.
   d. do not nourish their young with milk.

_____ **8.** In which of the following mammals does an embryo spend the most time developing inside the mother?
   a. echidna   c. kangaroo
   b. elephant   d. koala

_____ 9. Proboscideans are mammals that
    a. have sharp teeth and claws.
    b. have trunks.
    c. spend most of their time underwater.
    d. have a single pair of long, curved incisors.

_____10. The similarities in body structure between an anteater and an aardvark are the result of
    a. climate changes.
    b. habitat destruction.
    c. convergent evolution.
    d. adaptive radiation.

_____11. Having a thumb that can move against the other fingers makes it possible for a primate to
    a. hold objects firmly.
    b. merge visual images.
    c. display elaborate social behaviors.
    d. judge the locations of tree branches.

_____12. A primate that uses its prehensile tail to swing from branch to branch is the
    a. gibbon.
    b. squirrel monkey.
    c. macaque.
    d. orangutan.

_____13. Hominids differ from other primates on the basis of all of the following EXCEPT
    a. brain size.
    b. method of reproduction.
    c. method of locomotion.
    d. shape of the hip bones.

_____14. Fossil evidence indicates that *Australopithecus afarensis*
    a. was primarily a meat-eater.
    b. had a large brain.
    c. was bipedal.
    d. appeared later than *Homo ergaster*.

_____15. The earliest hominid that belonged to the same genus as modern humans was probably
    a. *Homo habilis.*
    b. *Homo neanderthalensis.*
    c. *Homo afarensis.*
    d. *Homo ergaster.*

Name_____ Class_____ Date_____

Completion

Complete each statement on the line provided.

16. Two features that are found in all mammals but not in any other chordates are hair and _____ .

17. Early mammals were probably nocturnal and ate _____ .

18. In placental mammals, nutrients, oxygen, carbon dioxide, and wastes are exchanged between the embryo and the mother through the _____ .

19. Hominids walk on two feet. This manner of walking is called _____ locomotion.

20. The group of primates called _____ includes New World monkeys, Old World monkeys, and hominoids.

Short Answer

In complete sentences, write the answers to the questions on the lines provided.

21. How can mammals be distinguished from other vertebrates on the basis of the fossils they leave behind?

_____

_____

_____

22. Explain the function of the rumen. Why is this organ absent in carnivores?

_____

_____

_____

23. What are two ways in which mammals maintain homeostasis?

_____

_____

_____

24. Explain how young marsupials complete their development.

_____

_____

_____

25. Why is binocular vision important to a primate that moves through the branches of trees?

_____

_____

_____

Using Science Skills

Use the diagram below to answer the following questions on the lines provided.

Hippopotamus   Rhinoceros   Bat   Whale

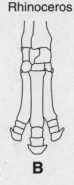   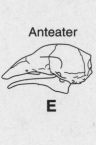

Anteater

A   B   C   D

E

Figure 1

26. **Applying Concepts** Drawing A shows the bones in the hoof of a hippopotamus. To which order does this mammal belong?

_____

_____

_____

27. **Applying Concepts** Drawing B shows bones in the hoof of a rhinoceros. To which order does this mammal belong?

_____

_____

_____

28. **Inferring** Drawing C shows bones in the wing of a bat. How is the structure of the limb adapted to flight?

_____

_____

_____

29. **Observing** Drawing D shows bones in the flipper of a whale. How does its bone structure differ from that of a bat?

_____

_____

30. **Inferring** Drawing E shows the skull of an anteater. How is the structure of this skull adapted to the anteater's diet?

_____

_____

Essay

Write the answer to each question in the space provided.

31. What adaptations do mammals have that enable them to maintain a constant body temperature?

32. Why is it important for mammals to have specialized teeth and digestive systems based on their diet?

33. Why are monotremes sometimes said to be intermediate between reptiles and most mammals in their manner of reproduction?

34. Compare and contrast New World monkeys and Old World monkeys

35. Explain how paleontologists have changed their views on early hominid evolution. What caused them to change their way of thinking?

Multiple Choice

Write the letter that best answers the question or completes the statement on the line provided.

____ 1. Mammals are characterized by each of the following EXCEPT
   a. three-chambered hearts.
   b. hair.
   c. endothermy.

____ 2. The first true mammals appeared during the
   a. Permian Period.
   b. late Triassic Period.
   c. Cretaceous Period.

____ 3. Mammals that have broad, flattened molars feed on
   a. plants.
   b. meat.
   c. plankton.

____ 4. Which body system includes the rumen?
   a. respiratory
   b. circulatory
   c. digestive

____ 5. In mammals, the amount of water in the body is controlled mainly by the
   a. kidneys.
   b. diaphragm.
   c. lungs.

____ 6. The egg-laying mammals are called
   a. marsupials.
   b. monotremes.
   c. placental mammals.

____ 7. An example of an animal with a marsupium is a(an)
   a. elephant.
   b. sea lion.
   c. wombat.

____ 8. The function of a placenta is to
   a. exchange materials between an embryo and its mother.
   b. store and process newly swallowed plant food.
   c. store urine until it is eliminated from the body.

_____ **9.** Which of the following mammals is a chiropteran?

    a. shrew

    b. rabbit

    c. bat

_____**10.** The similar appearance of armadillos and aardvarks is an example of

    a. continental drift.

    b. convergent evolution.

    c. social interaction.

_____**11.** Which of the following is NOT a characteristic of most primates?

    a. opposable digits

    b. a well-developed cerebrum

    c. a cloaca

_____**12.** An example of a prosimian is a(an)

    a. lemur.

    b. baboon.

    c. orangutan.

_____**13.** Bipedal locomotion consists of

    a. swinging from branch to branch.

    b. using the tail to grasp branches during walking.

    c. walking on two feet.

_____**14.** Which of the following was a characteristic of *Homo habilis*?

    a. using tools made of stone and bone

    b. producing cave paintings

    c. having a skeleton similar to that of a gorilla

_____**15.** Which statement is true of the Neanderthals?

    a. They evolved after the Cro-Magnons.

    b. They made stone tools.

    c. They became extinct about 1 million years ago.

Name_____ Class_____ Date _____

Completion

Complete each statement on the line provided.

16. Mammals have _____ and body fat that help conserve body heat.

17. The only monotremes that exist today are the _____ and the spiny anteaters.

18. Primates can display more complex behaviors than many other mammals because they have a well-developed _____ .

19. The anthropoids that are native to Central and South America are called _____ monkeys.

20. A(An) _____ thumb enables primates to grasp objects.

Short Answer

In complete sentences, write the answers to the questions on the lines provided.

21. Name the four specialized types of mammalian teeth.

_____

_____

_____

22. What is the function of the diaphragm?

_____

_____

_____

23. What are the most important characteristics that scientists use to classify mammals into subgroups?

_____

_____

24. What is a marsupium?

_____

_____

_____

25. What is a prosimian?

_____

_____

_____

Using Science Skills

Use the diagrams below to answer the following questions on the lines provided.

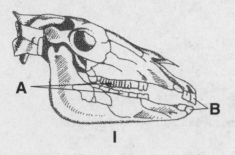 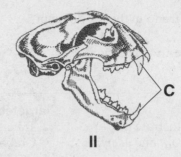

I   II

Figure 1

26. **Inferring** Which skull—I or II—in Figure 1 is that of a carnivore and which is that of a herbivore?

_____

_____

27. **Interpreting Graphics** Identify the teeth labeled A and describe their function in this mammal.

_____

_____

28. **Interpreting Graphics** Identify the teeth labeled B and describe their function in this mammal.

_____

_____

_____

29. **Interpreting Graphics** Identify the teeth labeled C and describe their function in this mammal.

_____

_____

_____

30. **Inferring** Describe how the jaws move when each mammal in Figure 1 chews its food.

_____

_____

_____

LESSON PLAN 33–1 (pages 849–852)

Chordate Evolution

Time
1 period
1/2 block

Section Objectives

- **33.1.1 Explain** what the roots of the chordate family tree are.
- **33.1.2 Summarize** a main trend in the evolution of chordates.

Vocabulary notochord • adaptive radiation

Local Standards

1 FOCUS

Vocabulary Preview
Students draw diagrams to illustrate the meanings of the words *notochord* and *adaptive radiation*.

Targeted Resources
- ❑ Transparencies: **485** Section 33–1 Interest Grabber
- ❑ Transparencies: **486** Section 33–1 Outline
- ❑ Transparencies: **487** Concept Map

2 INSTRUCT

Make Connections: Earth Science
Explain how Burgess Shale fossils were formed.
L2

Use Visuals: Figure 33–2
Use Figure 33–2 to help students interpret the cladogram showing the phylogenetic relationships of chordates. **L1 L2**

Build Science Skills: Using Models
Students develop skits to model adaptive radiation and convergent evolution. **L2**

Build Science Skills: Applying Concepts
Students identify other examples of convergent evolution in the chordate family tree. **L2**

Use Visuals: Figure 33–4
Help students interpret the pie chart showing the diversity of chordates in Figure 33–4.
L1 L2

Targeted Resources
- ❑ Reading and Study Workbook: Section 33–1
- ❑ Adapted Reading and Study Workbook: Section 33–1
- ❑ Transparencies: **488** Figure 33–2 A Cladogram of Chordates, **489** Figure 33–4 Diversity of Chordates
- ❑ Teaching Resources: Section Summaries 33–1. Worksheets 33–1, Enrichment
- ❑ Lab Worksheets: Chapter 33 Exploration
- ❑ **NSTA** *sci*$_{LINKS}$ Chordates

3 ASSESS

Evaluate Understanding
Students draw a family tree to show the relationships among the chordate groups.

Reteach
Students develop a concept map that shows the major trends in chordate evolution.

Targeted Resources
- ❑ Teaching Resources: Section Review 33–1
- ❑ **i Text** Section 33–1

LESSON PLAN 33–2 (pages 854–856)

Time
1 period
1/2 block

Controlling Body Temperature

Section Objectives

- **33.2.1 Explain** how the control of body temperature is an important aspect of vertebrate life.
- **33.2.2 Contrast** ectotherms and endotherms.

Vocabulary ectotherm • endotherm

Local Standards

---

1 FOCUS

Reading Strategy
Have students take notes in a compare-and-contrast table about endotherms and ectotherms.

Targeted Resources
❑ Transparencies: **490** Section 33–2 Interest Grabber
❑ Transparencies: **491** Section 33–2 Outline

---

2 INSTRUCT

Use Visuals: Figure 33–5
Use Figure 33–5 to discuss how the penguins in the photograph maintain homeostasis. **L1 L2**

Analyzing Data
Students analyze data about temperature control in different chordates. **L2**

Build Science Skills: Making Judgments
Students debate the pros and cons of ectothermy. **L2**

Build Science Skills: Formulating Hypotheses
Students hypothesize how endothermy first evolved. **L2 L3**

Targeted Resources
❑ Reading and Study Workbook: Section 33–2
❑ Adapted Reading and Study Workbook: Section 33–2
❑ Teaching Resources: Section Summaries 33–2, Worksheets 33–2
❑ Transparencies: **492** Temperature Control in Chordates
❑ **NSTA** *sci*LINKS Homeostasis

---

3 ASSESS

Evaluate Understanding
Quiz students about the features of body temperature control.

Reteach
Students create a Venn diagram to compare and contrast endothermy and ectothermy.

Targeted Resources
Teaching Resources: Section Review 33–2
❑ *i*Text Section 33–2

Teacher_____ Class_____ Date_____ M T W T F

LESSON PLAN 33–3 (pages 857–864)

Form and Function in Chordates

Time
2 periods
1 block

Section Objective

- **33.3.1 Describe** how the organ systems of the different groups of chordates carry out essential life functions.

Vocabulary alveolus

Local Standards

1 FOCUS

Vocabulary Preview
Explain how Latin words such as *alveolus* are made plural.

Targeted Resources
❏ Transparencies: **493** Section 33–3 Interest Grabber

❏ Transparencies: **494** Section 33–3 Outline

❏ Transparencies: **495** Compare/Contrast Table

2 INSTRUCT

Use Visuals: Figure 33–8
Students use Figure 33–8 to compare and contrast the digestive systems of vertebrates.
L1 L2

Demonstration
Students indirectly observe how ridges and folds increase the surface of the lungs. **L2**

Build Science Skills: Forming Operational Definitions
Students develop rules that relate the structural complexity of the circulatory system to its function in all chordate groups. **L2 L3**

Address Misconceptions
Dispel the misconception that humans have the best-developed senses. **L2**

Make Connections: Physics
Compare the lines of force in the two types of vertebrate stances. **L2**

Build Science Skills: Comparing and Contrasting
Students compare and contrast the three modes of development in vertebrates. **L1 L2**

Targeted Resources
❏ Reading and Study Workbook: Section 33–3

❏ Adapted Reading and Study Workbook: Section 33–3

❏ Teaching Resources: Section Summaries 33–3, Worksheets 33–3

❏ Transparencies: **496** Figure 33–8 Digestive Systems of Vertebrates, **497** Figure 33–10 Vertebrate Lungs, **498** Figure 33–11 The Circulatory System of Vertebrates

❏ Lab Manual A: Chapter 33 Lab

❏ Lab Manual B: Chapter 33 Lab

❏ **PHSchool.com** Career links

3 ASSESS

Evaluate Understanding
Play a game of Jeopardy™ to review the seven organ systems in the chordate groups.

Reteach
Student pairs interview each other about the structures and functions of the various organ systems.

Targeted Resources
❏ Teaching Resources: Section Review 33–3, Chapter Vocabulary Review, Graphic Organizer, Chapter 33 Tests: Levels A and B

❏ **iText** Section 33–3, Chapter 33 Assessment

❏ **PHSchool.com** Online Chapter 33 Test

Chapter 33   Comparing Chordates

Summary

33–1 Chordate Evolution

Embryo studies of living chordates help scientists learn about chordate evolution. In addition, evidence of early chordates was found in the fossilized remains of an organism called *Pikaia*. *Pikaia* had a notochord and paired muscles.

Chordates include vertebrates and nonvertebrates. **In the chordate family tree, vertebrates, tunicates, and lancelets share a common ancestor.** Modern amphibians, reptiles, birds, and mammals share more recent common ancestors.

Scientists infer how vertebrates evolved by studying fossils and the features of living chordates. **Over the course of evolution, the appearance of new adaptations—such as jaws and paired appendages—has launched adaptive radiations in chordate groups. Adaptive radiation** brings about new species with unlike adaptations. These species look different, but are related. The finches that Darwin studied are good examples of adaptive radiation. More than a dozen different finch species evolved from one species. Convergent evolution has also occurred many times during chordate evolution. **Convergent evolution** occurs when unrelated species adapt to similar environments. Convergent evolution results in unrelated species that look and behave alike. For example, convergent evolution has led to the development of birds and bats. Both can fly, but they are very different types of organisms.

33–2 Controlling Body Temperature

The control of body temperature is important for maintaining homeostasis in vertebrates. To control temperature, vertebrates need a source of body heat, a way to conserve heat, and a way to get rid of excess heat. In terms of how they generate heat, vertebrates can be classified into two groups: ectotherms and endotherms.

- Most reptiles, fishes, and amphibians are ectotherms. **Ectotherms are animals whose body temperatures are controlled primarily by taking heat from, or losing heat to, the environment.** Ectotherms have low metabolic rates. They also lack good insulation and easily lose heat to the environment.
- **Endotherms** make their own body heat. **Birds and mammals are endotherms, which means that they can generate and retain heat inside their bodies.** They have high metabolic rates. They have fat and outer coverings—such as feathers or hair—to keep heat within their bodies. They get rid of excess heat by sweating or panting.

33–3 Form and Function in Chordates

Organ systems of different vertebrates are specialized to perform specific functions. These systems become more complex from fishes to mammals.

Digestion. Vertebrates have adaptations for eating a variety of foods. For example, the hummingbird's long bill and the honey possum's narrow snout are adaptations for feeding on nectar. Carnivores have sharp teeth that help them tear chunks of meat from their prey. **The digestive systems of vertebrates have organs that are well adapted for different feeding habits.** Herbivores have long digestive tracts. In addition, herbivores often have stomachs that house bacteria to help break down plant fibers.

Respiration. **Chordates have two basic respiratory plans: some use gills; others have lungs.**
- Water animals (tunicates, fishes, and amphibian larvae) use gills for respiration.
- Land animals (adult amphibians, reptiles, birds, and mammals) use lungs.

The efficiency of the lungs increases as you move from amphibians to reptiles to mammals. Birds have the most efficient respiratory system of all the vertebrates. Their air sacs and tubes ensure that oxygen-rich air is always in the lungs.

Circulation. **As chordates evolved, the heart developed chambers and partitions that helped to separate oxygen-rich blood from oxygen-poor blood.**
- Fish have two chambers: an atrium to receive blood from the body and a ventricle to pump blood.
- Amphibians have three chambers: two atria and one ventricle. Oxygen-rich and oxygen-poor blood mix in the ventricle.
- Most reptiles also have a three-chambered heart. However, the ventricle has a partial partition. This partition reduces the amount that oxygen-rich and oxygen-poor blood mix.
- Birds, mammals, and crocodiles have a four-chambered heart. Oxygen-rich blood is completely separated from oxygen-poor blood.

Vertebrates with gills have a single-loop circulatory system. Blood travels from the heart to the gills, to the rest of the body, and back to the heart. Vertebrates with lungs have a double-loop circulatory system. The first loop moves blood between the heart and the lungs. The second loop moves blood between the heart and the body.

<u>Excretion</u>. The excretory system removes nitrogenous wastes from the body. It also controls the amount of water in the body.

- In nonvertebrate chordates and fishes, wastes in the form of ammonia diffuse out of the body through gills and gill slits.
- In most other vertebrates, kidneys filter wastes from the blood. Land vertebrates excrete wastes as urea or uric acid. This type of excretion helps these animals conserve water.

<u>Response</u>. **Nonvertebrate chordates have fairly simple nervous systems.** They do not have specialized sense organs. **Vertebrates have more complex brains.** Each region of the brain is distinct and has its own function. The sense organs and nerve cells in vertebrates are mostly at the front of the body. From fishes to mammals, the size and complexity of the cerebrum and cerebellum increase.

<u>Movement</u>. Vertebrates are more mobile than nonvertebrate chordates. All vertebrates, except jawless fishes, have an internal skeleton of bone, or in some fishes, cartilage. The bones are held together with tough, flexible tissues. These tissues allow movement and keep the bones in place. **The skeletal and muscular systems support a vertebrate's body and make it possible to control movement.** Amphibians have limbs that stick out sideways. Reptiles, birds, and mammals have limbs directly under the body. This placement supports more body weight.

<u>Reproduction</u>. Most chordates reproduce sexually. Fishes and amphibians have external fertilization. The eggs of reptiles, birds, and mammals are fertilized internally. Chordates may be oviparous, ovoviviparous, or viviparous.

- In oviparous species, eggs develop outside the mother's body. Most fishes, amphibians, reptiles, and all birds are oviparous.
- In ovoviviparous species like sharks, eggs develop inside the mother's body. The embryo gets nutrients from the egg yolk. The young are born alive.
- In viviparous species, which include most mammals, embryos get nutrients directly from the mother.

Chordate Adaptations

The cladogram shows the relationships between modern chordates. Some important adaptations that have occurred during chordate evolution are indicated.

Follow the prompts to analyze the cladogram.
- Color the bar for chordates without vertebrae red.
- Color the bars for chordates that have jaws but no lungs blue.
- Color the bars for chordates that have lungs yellow.

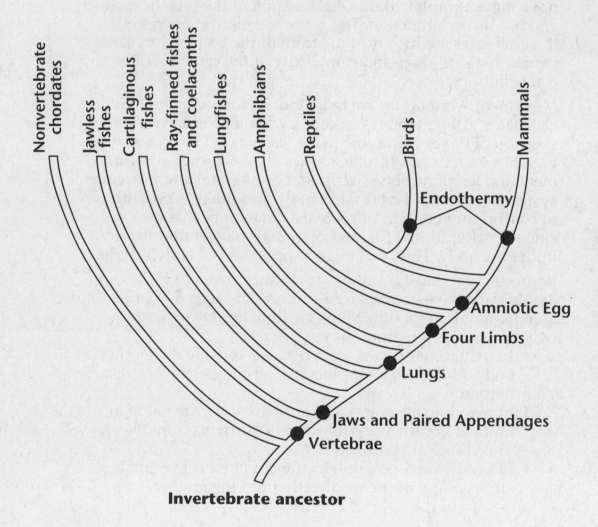

Use the cladogram to answer the questions.

1. Which chordates are endotherms?

_____

2. Which chordates are most closely related to reptiles?

_____

Ectotherms and Endotherms

Ectotherms are animals whose body temperature is mostly determined by the temperature of the environment. Endotherms are animals that can regulate their own body temperatures. Most reptiles, fishes, and amphibians are ectotherms. Birds and mammals are endotherms.

Use what you know about ectotherms and endotherms to complete the table. Write how the animal's body temperature will change in response to the environmental change. Write increase, decrease, *or* stay the same. *One row has been completed for you.*

Animal	Environmental Temperature Change	Body Temperature Change
turtle	increase	increase
salamander	decrease	
eagle	decrease	
alligator	increase	
rabbit	increase	
goldfish	decrease	

Use the table to answer the questions.

1. What happens to an endotherm's body temperature when the environmental temperature increases?

_____

2. What happens to an ectotherm's body temperature when the environmental temperature decreases?

_____

Vertebrate Digestive Systems

Vertebrates have digestive systems adapted for the foods they eat. Most vertebrates, however, have some similar digestive organs.

Look at the diagram of the salamander. Find the esophagus, liver, stomach, *and* intestine. *Then color the other diagrams according to the prompts below.*

- Color the esophagus yellow.
- Color the liver orange.
- Color the intestine red.

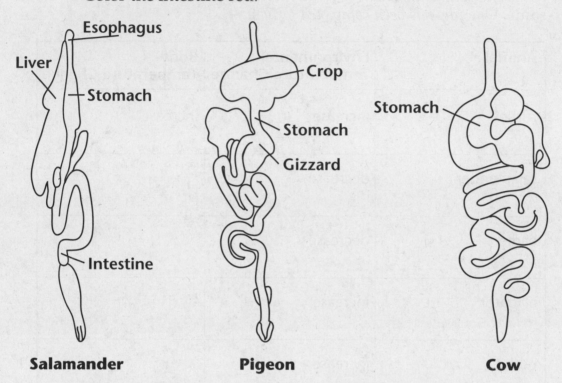

Salamander   **Pigeon**   **Cow**

Answer the questions.

1. Cows are herbivores. What might the bacteria in the intestines of cows do? Circle the correct answer.

   break down plant tissue   produce meat-digesting enzymes

2. How might the cow's intestines be different if a cow were a carnivore?

   _____

   _____

3. Why does the pigeon need a crop and gizzard?

   _____

   _____

Respiratory Systems of Land Vertebrates

Land vertebrates use lungs to breathe. In most land vertebrates, air moves in and out through the same passageways, including the nostrils, mouth, throat, and trachea.

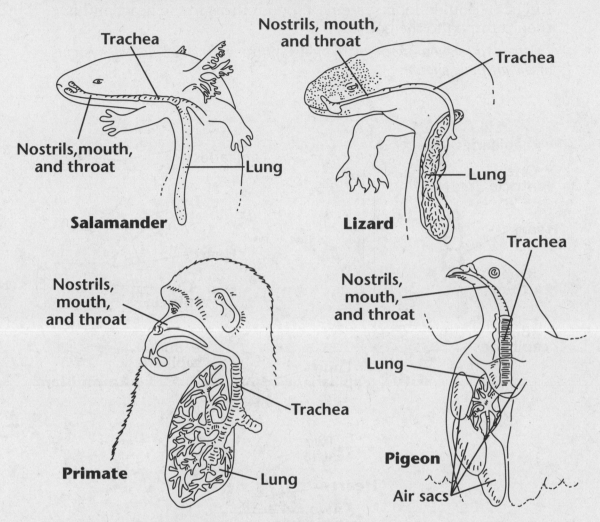

Use the diagrams to answer the questions.

1. How are salamander and lizard lungs different?

_____

_____

2. In mammalian lungs, gas exchange takes place in which structures? Circle the correct answer.

    lungs   gills

3. What is the function of air sacs in the pigeon?

_____

_____

Vertebrate Circulatory Systems

Vertebrates that use gills have single-loop circulatory systems.
Vertebrates that use lungs have double-loop circulatory systems.
In a single-loop system, the heart pumps blood to the gills or
lungs. In double-loop systems, blood returns to the heart and is
then pumped to the body.

*Draw arrows showing the path of blood through the circulatory systems
of the animals shown.*

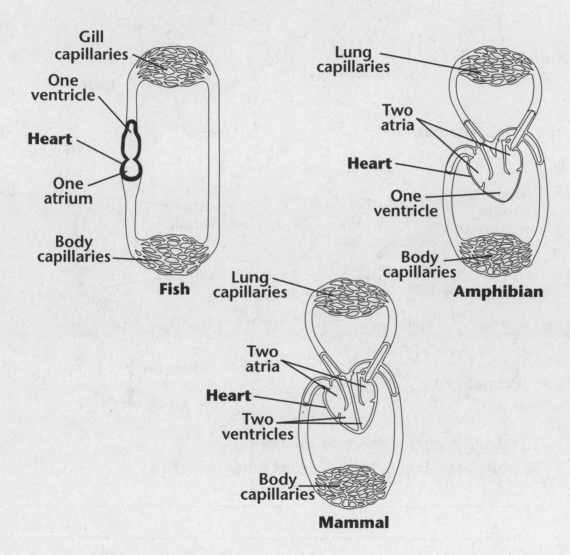

Use the diagrams to answer the question.

1. Which vertebrate shown has the simplest circulatory system?

_____

Vertebrate Brains

Vertebrates have complex brains made up of several parts. Each part has a different function. For example, the medulla oblongata controls the functioning of many internal organs.

Look at the diagrams of the bony fish and amphibian brains. Then color the remaining diagrams according to the prompts below.

- Color the olfactory bulb purple.
- Color the optic lobe blue.
- Color the medulla oblongata yellow.
- Color the cerebellum red.
- Color the cerebrum orange.

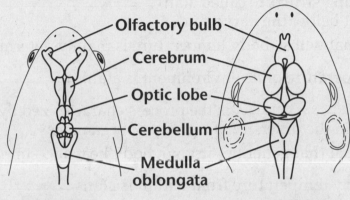

Olfactory bulb
Cerebrum
Optic lobe
Cerebellum
Medulla oblongata

Bony Fish   **Amphibian**

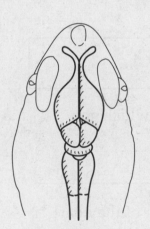

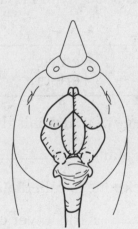

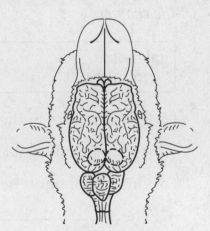

Reptile   **Bird**   **Mammal**

Use the diagrams to answer the question.

1. Which vertebrate has the most complex cerebrum?

_____

Chapter 33   Comparing Chordates

Vocabulary Review

Completion   *Use the words below to fill in the blanks with terms from the chapter.*

adaptive radiation	endotherm
ectotherm	notochord

1. All chordates, at some stage of life, have a long, flexible, supporting structure called a(an) _____ that runs just below the nerve cord.

2. An animal whose body temperature is mainly determined by the temperature of its environment is a(an) _____.

3. _____ is the process characterized by rapid growth in the diversity of a group of organisms.

4. An animal that generates its own body heat and controls its own body temperature from within is a(an) _____.

Completion   *Use the words below to fill in the blanks with terms from the chapter.*

alveolus	ventricle
cerebrum	vertebra

5. The structure in the lungs of mammals through which gas exchange takes place is a(an) _____.

6. One segment of the backbone is called a(an) _____.

7. The _____ is the lower chamber of the heart that pumps blood.

8. In most vertebrates, the _____ is responsible for voluntary activities of the body.

Summary

33–1 Chordate Evolution

Scientists have learned the most about chordates by studying the embryos of living organisms. Scientists have found evidence of early chordates in the fossilized remains of *Pikaia*. *Pikaia* had a notochord and paired muscles. On the basis of this early evidence, scientists classify *Pikaia* as an early chordate.

Chordates include both vertebrates and nonvertebrates. These two groups share a common invertebrate ancestor. Modern amphibians, reptiles, birds, and mammals share more recent common ancestors.

Scientists infer how vertebrates have evolved by studying fossils and the characteristics of living chordates. Scientists believe that the appearance of new adaptations, such as jaws and paired appendages, has led to adaptive radiations. Adaptive radiation results in many new species with different adaptations. Even though these species might look different, they are related.

Another trend in evolution, called convergent evolution, occurs when unrelated species adapt to similar environments. Convergent evolution produces species that look and behave alike even though they are not related.

33–2 Controlling Body Temperature

Controlling body temperature is important for maintaining homeostasis. The chemical reactions that carry out life functions can occur only within a certain temperature range. Vertebrates have different ways to control body temperature. These ways depend on a source of body heat, a way to conserve heat, and a way to get rid of excess heat.

In terms of how they generate and control their body heat, vertebrates are classified into two basic groups: ectotherms and endotherms. Ectotherms rely on the temperature of the environment for body heat. Ectotherms have low rates of metabolism. They do not have good insulation and easily lose heat to the environment.

Endotherms generate their own body heat. They have high metabolic rates. They conserve heat within their bodies with outer coverings, such as feathers, fat, and fur or hair. They get rid of excess heat by sweating or panting.

Endotherms can survive in cool temperatures. However, they require a lot of food. Ectotherms need much less food. However, they cannot survive in very cold environments.

The first land vertebrates were most likely ectotherms. Scientists do not know exactly when endothermy evolved. Some scientists think that dinosaurs were endotherms; others do not. Evidence suggests that endothermy might have evolved more than once.

33–3 Form and Function in Chordates

Organ systems of different vertebrates are specialized to perform specific functions. The complexity of these systems increases from fishes to mammals.

The skulls and teeth of vertebrates are adapted for feeding on a wide variety of foods. For example, the hummingbird's long bill and the narrow snout of the honey possum are adaptations for feeding on nectar. Invertebrates' digestive systems are also adapted for different feeding habits. Carnivores have shorter digestive tracts than herbivores. Herbivores often house bacteria to help break down plant fibers.

Chordates have two basic structures for respiration. Animals that live in water use gills for respiration. Animals that live on land use lungs. As you move from amphibians to mammals, the surface area of the lungs increases. Birds have the most efficient gas exchange. The combination of air sacs and tubes ensures that oxygen-rich air is always in the lungs.

Vertebrates with gills have a single-loop circulatory system. Blood travels from the heart to the gills, then to the rest of the body, and back to the heart. Vertebrates with lungs have a double-loop circulatory system. The first loop carries blood between the heart and the lungs. The second loop carries blood between the heart and the body.

As chordates evolved, the heart developed chambers to separate oxygen-rich blood from oxygen-poor blood. Fish have two chambers: an atrium to receive blood from the body and a ventricle to pump blood. Amphibians have three chambers: two atria and one ventricle. Most reptiles also have a three-chambered heart, but the ventricle has a partial partition. Birds, mammals, and crocodiles have a four-chambered heart. Oxygen-rich blood is completely separated from oxygen-poor blood.

The excretory system removes nitrogenous wastes from the body. It also controls the amount of water in the body. In nonvertebrate chordates and fishes, wastes leave the body through gills and gill slits. These wastes are in the form of ammonia. In most other vertebrates, the kidneys filter out wastes. Vertebrates that live on land excrete wastes in less toxic forms such as urea or uric acid. This enables land vertebrates to conserve water.

Nonvertebrate chordates have a relatively simple nervous system. They do not have specialized sense organs. Vertebrates have a much more complex brain. Each region of the brain is distinct and has a different function. The sense organs and nerve cells in vertebrates are concentrated at the front of the body. From fishes to mammals, the size and complexity of the cerebrum and cerebellum increase.

Vertebrates are much more mobile than nonvertebrate chordates. All vertebrates, except jawless fishes, have an internal skeleton of bone, or in some fishes, cartilage. The bones are held together with tough, flexible tissues that allow movement and keep the bones in place. Body muscles and limb placement help vertebrates move. Amphibians have limbs that stick out sideways. Reptiles, birds, and mammals have limbs directly under the body. This supports more body weight.

Almost all chordates reproduce sexually. Fishes and amphibians have external fertilization. The eggs of reptiles, birds, and mammals are fertilized internally.

Chordates may be oviparous, ovoviviparous, or viviparous. In oviparous species, the eggs develop outside the mother's body. Most fishes, amphibians, reptiles, and all birds are oviparous. In ovoviviparous species like sharks, the eggs develop inside the mother's body. The embryo gets nutrients from the egg yolk. The young are born alive. In viviparous species like most mammals, the embryos get nutrients directly from the mother. Like ovoviviparous species, the young of viviparous animals are born alive.

Chapter 33 Comparing Chordates

Section 33–1 Chordate Evolution (pages 849–852)

🔑 Key Concepts

- What are the roots of the chordate family tree?
- What is a main trend in the evolution of chordates?

Chordate Origins (page 849)

1. Studies of embryos of living organisms suggest that the most ancient chordates were closely related to _____.

2. Why do scientists consider *Pikaia* to be an early chordate and not a worm?

_____

_____

3. In the diagram below, label the notochord, head region, paired muscle blocks, tentacle, and tail fin of *Pikaia*.

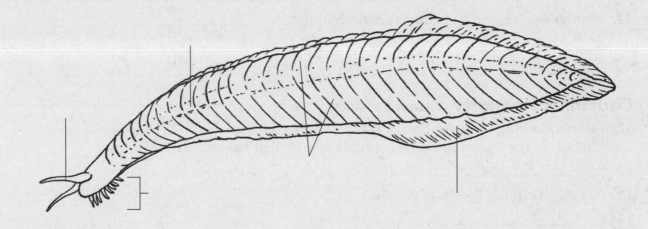

4. A flexible, supporting structure found only in chordates is a(an) _____.

5. Is the following question true or false? Scientists study tunicate larvae to better understand the early evolution of chordates. _____

The Chordate Family Tree (page 850)

6. Circle the letter of each sentence that is true about the chordate family tree. (See Figure 33–2 on page 850 of your textbook.)

   a. Vertebrates share a common invertebrate ancestor with tunicates and lancelets.

   b. Mammals and fishes share a more recent common ancestor than mammals and birds.

   c. Lungs evolved before paired appendages.

   d. Endothermy evolved after the amniotic egg.

Evolutionary Trends in Vertebrates (page 851)

7. What two things do scientists use to study the evolutionary trends in vertebrates?

   a. _____

   b. _____

8. What effect has the appearance of new adaptations had on the evolution of

   vertebrates? _____

   _____

   _____

   _____

9. What is convergent evolution? _____

   _____

   _____

10. When does convergent evolution occur? _____

    _____

    _____

11. What is one example of convergent evolution? _____

    _____

    _____

Chordate Diversity (pages 851–852)

12. Is the following sentence true or false? The chordate species alive today are a small fraction of the total number of chordate species that have existed over time.

    _____

13. List the six living chordate groups.

    a. _____

    b. _____

    c. _____

    d. _____

    e. _____

    f. _____

Reading Skill Practice

By looking carefully at photographs and illustrations in textbooks, you can help yourself better understand what you have read. Look carefully at Figure 33–3 on page 851 in your textbook. What idea does the photograph communicate?

Section 33–2 Controlling Body Temperature
(pages 854–856)

👓 **Key Concepts**
- How is the control of body temperature an important aspect of vertebrate life?
- What is the difference between ectotherms and endotherms?

Body Temperature and Homeostasis (pages 854–855)

1. Circle the letter of each sentence that is true about body temperature.

   a. Essential life functions in animals can be carried out most efficiently at any temperature.

   b. If muscles are too cold, they may contract slowly.

   c. If an animal gets too hot, its muscles will work more efficiently.

   d. The control of body temperature is important for maintaining homeostasis.

2. List three features that vertebrates need in order to control their body temperature.

   a. _____

   b. _____

   c. _____

Match each description with the method of controlling body heat. Methods may be used more than once.

	Description	Method
_____	**3.** An animal whose body temperature is controlled from within	**a.** Ectotherm
_____	**4.** Examples include reptiles, fishes, and amphibians	**b.** Endotherm
_____	**5.** Warm up by basking in the sun	
_____	**6.** High metabolic rates that generate a significant amount of heat	
_____	**7.** An animal whose body temperature is mainly determined by the temperature of its environment	
_____	**8.** Have feathers, body fat, or hair for insulation	
_____	**9.** Easily lose heat to the environment	
_____	**10.** Low metabolic rate	
_____	**11.** Cools off by panting or sweating	

Comparing Ectotherms and Endotherms (page 856)

12. Name one advantage and one disadvantage of endothermy.

Advantage: _____

_____

Disadvantage: _____

_____

13. Is the following sentence true or false? Ectothermy is a more energy-efficient way to live in cold environments. _____

Evolution of Temperature Control (page 856)

14. Circle the letter of each sentence that is true about the evolution of temperature control.

    a. The first land vertebrates were ectotherms.

    b. Scientists know when endothermy evolved.

    c. Some biologists hypothesize that dinosaurs were endotherms.

    d. Evidence suggests that endothermy evolved more than once.

Section 33–3 Form and Function in Chordates
(pages 857–864)

Key Concept
- How do the organ systems of the different groups of chordates carry out essential life functions?

Feeding (pages 857–858)

1. Most tunicates and all lancelets are _____. They remove plankton from the water that passes through their _____.

2. Circle the letter of the vertebrates that are filter feeders.

   a. tunicates   **b.** flamingoes   **c.** manta rays   **d.** crocodiles

3. What adaptations do vertebrates have to feed on nectar? _____
_____

4. Is the following sentence true or false? Mammals with sharp canine teeth and incisors are filter feeders. _____

5. Circle the letter of the vertebrates that typically have short digestive tracts that produce enzymes.

   a. herbivores   **b.** endotherms   **c.** carnivores   **d.** ectotherms

Respiration (pages 858–859)

6. Is the following sentence true or false? Generally, aquatic chordates use lungs for respiration. _____

7. List three examples of respiratory adaptations or structures used by chordates in addition to gills and lungs.

   a. _____
   _____

   b. _____
   _____

   c. _____

8. Describe the basic process of breathing among land vertebrates. _____
_____
_____
_____
_____

9. Is the following sentence true or false? Mammals typically have more surface area in their lungs than amphibians. _____

10. Bubblelike structures in the lungs that provide an enormous surface area for gas exchange are called _____.

11. Complete the flowchart that describes the path of water as it moves through a fish. See Figure 33–9 on page 859.

> Water flows in through the fish's _____, where muscles pump the water across the _____.

⬇

> As water passes over the gill filaments, _____ molecules diffuse into blood in the capillaries. At the same time, _____ diffuses from blood into water.

⬇

> Water and carbon dioxide are pumped out through the _____.

12. Why do mammals need large amounts of oxygen? _____
_____
_____

13. Why are the lungs of birds most efficient? _____
_____
_____

Circulation (pages 860–861)

14. Is the following sentence true or false? Chordates that use gills for respiration have a single-loop circulatory system. _____

15. Identify where the blood is carried in each loop of a double-loop circulatory system.
First loop: _____
Second loop: _____

16. Is the following sentence true or false? In a double-loop system, oxygen-poor blood from the heart is carried to the body. _____

17. In vertebrates with gills, the heart consists of _____

18. What is the advantage of the reptilian heart over the amphibian heart? _____
_____
_____

19. Why is a four-chambered heart sometimes described as a double pump? _____
_____

Excretion (page 861)

20. In nonvertebrate chordates and fishes, _____ play an important role in excretion. However, most vertebrates rely on _____ .

21. Circle the letter of each chordate that eliminates nitrogenous wastes as urea.

    a. tunicates   c. birds

    b. reptiles   d. mammals

22. How do vertebrate kidneys help maintain homeostasis? _____
   _____
   _____

Response (page 862)

23. Is the following sentence true or false? Nonvertebrate chordates have a complex brain with distinct regions. _____

24. Circle the letter of the part of the brain that controls the function of many internal organs.

    a. medulla oblongata   c. olfactory bulbs

    b. optic lobes   d. cerebrum

25. Is the following sentence true or false? The cerebrum and cerebellum are most developed in birds and mammals. _____

Movement (page 863)

26. Although nonvertebrate chordates lack bones, they do have _____ .

27. What structures make it possible for vertebrates to control movement? _____
   _____
   _____

Reproduction (page 864)

28. Is the following sentence true or false? Vertebrate evolution shows a general trend from internal to external fertilization. _____

29. Circle the letter of development in which the eggs develop internally and the embryos receive nutrients from the yolk surrounding them.

    a. oviparous   c. viviparous

    b. ovoviviparous   d. asexual

Vocabulary Review

Labeling Diagrams   *Study the diagrams of the vertebrate brains below. Then, write the vertebrate group to which each brain belongs.*

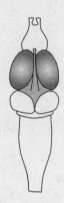   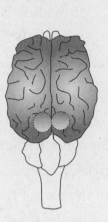 

_____   _____   _____   _____   _____

Multiple Choice   *In the space provided, write the letter of the answer that best completes each sentence or answers the question.*

_____ **6.** Which of the following best describes a notochord?
  a. develops into gills in fishes
  c. is dorsal and hollow
  b. is a flexible, supporting structure
  d. extends posterior to the anus

_____ **7.** The rapid diversification of species as they adapt to new conditions is
  a. adaptive radiation.
  c. convergent evolution.
  b. divergent evolution.
  d. homeostasis.

_____ **8.** Which of the following is NOT true about ectotherms?
  a. The environment determines their body temperature.
  b. These animals have low metabolic rates.
  c. Examples include birds and mammals.
  d. Examples include reptiles, fishes, and amphibians.

_____ **9.** Endotherms get rid of excess heat by
  a. seeking shelter in underground burrows.
  b. basking in the sun.
  c. fluffing up feathers.
  d. panting or sweating.

_____ **10.** Alveoli are located in the
  a. digestive system.
  c. circulatory system.
  b. brain.
  d. lungs.

Chapter 33 Comparing Chordates   **Section Review 33-1**

Reviewing Key Concepts

Short Answer *On the lines provided, answer the following questions.*

1. List four features found in all chordates at some point in their development.
   _____
   _____

2. What is considered the first chordate, and what led scientists to classify it as a chordate?
   _____
   _____

3. What are the two groups of chordates with which vertebrates share a common ancestor?
   _____

4. Over the course of evolution, what launched adaptive radiations in chordate groups?
   _____

5. List the following adaptations in the order in which they appeared during chordate evolution: lungs, jaws, vertebrae, endothermy, four limbs.
   _____

Completion *On the lines provided, complete the following sentences.*

6. The rapid diversification of species as they adapt to new conditions is called
   _____ .

7. The process that produces two species that are similar in appearance and behavior, but are not closely related, is called _____ .

8. About 96 percent of all living chordate species are classified as
   _____ .

Reviewing Key Skills

9. **Applying Concepts** How are the wings of bats and birds an example of convergent evolution?
   _____
   _____

10. **Posing Questions** What is an example of a question you would ask about a newly discovered species, in order to tell whether the species is a chordate?
    _____
    _____

Chapter 33 Comparing Chordates   **Section Review 33-2**

Reviewing Key Concepts

Short Answer *On the lines provided, answer the following questions.*

1. Explain the importance of controlling body temperature for an organism.

   _____

   _____

2. What are the three important features that all vertebrates incorporate into controlling body temperature?

   _____

   _____

Identification *On the lines provided, identify each description as a characteristic of an* endotherm *or an* ectotherm.

_____ 3. includes most fishes, reptiles, and amphibians

_____ 4. has a high rate of resting metabolism

_____ 5. may sweat to get rid of excess body heat

_____ 6. is more energy efficient in environments with constant warm temperatures

_____ 7. can move around easily at night and during cool weather

_____ 8. requires a large amount of food

Reviewing Key Skills

9. **Applying Concepts** Give examples of how an alligator would adjust to changes in environmental temperature.

   _____

   _____

   _____

   _____

   _____

10. **Comparing and Contrasting** How are the temperature-regulating systems of birds and mammals similar? How are they different?

   _____

   _____

   _____

   _____

   _____

Chapter 33 Comparing Chordates   **Section Review 33-3**

Reviewing Key Concepts

Short Answer *On the lines provided, answer the following questions.*

1. Describe the differences in the digestive tracts of carnivores and herbivores.

   _____

   _____

   _____

2. What are the two respiratory structures typically found in chordates?

   _____

3. What is the general function of chambers and partitions in the heart?

   _____

   _____

4. How do both gills and kidneys function in excretion?

   _____

   _____

   _____

5. Describe how the brain structure of nonvertebrate chordates is different
   from that of vertebrate chordates.

   _____

   _____

6. What structures support a vertebrate's body and allow it to control movement?

   _____

Reviewing Key Skills

Classifying *On the line below each diagram, classify the diagram as the
circulatory system found in a* fish, *an* amphibian, *or a* mammal.

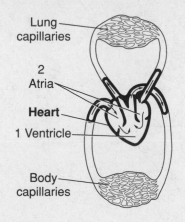 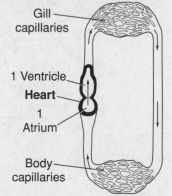 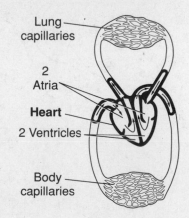

7. _____   8. _____   9. _____

Name_____ Class_____ Date_____

Defining Terms *On the lines provided, define each of the following terms.*

1. notochord _____
_____

2. adaptive radiation _____
_____

3. ectotherm _____
_____

4. endotherm _____
_____

5. alveolus _____
_____

6. single-loop circulatory system _____
_____

7. double-loop circulatory system _____
_____

Identifying Diagrams *On the line provided, identify each animal as an* ectotherm *or* endotherm.

8. _____   9. _____

10. _____   11. _____

12. _____

Multiple Choice *On the lines provided, write the letter that best completes the sentence or answers the question.*

_____ **13.** Scientists now consider *Pikaia* the first chordate because it

    a. was an ectotherm.   c. had adaptive radiation.

    b. was an endotherm.   d. had a notochord.

_____ **14.** An adaptive radiation often follows

    a. the appearance of new adaptations.   c. phylogenetic relationships.

    b. convergent evolution.   d. diversification.

_____ **15.** On a chilly day, a snake moves from the shade to a sunny rock. This behavior is characteristic of a(an)

    a. ectotherm.   c. chordate.

    b. endotherm.   d. vertebrate.

_____ **16.** Which term describes an animal that pants and sweats to help regulate its internal temperature?

    a. ectotherm   c. chordate

    b. endotherm   d. vertebrate

_____ **17.** Which organisms have relatively high metabolic rates?

    a. all animals   c. all vertebrates

    b. endotherms   d. ectotherms

_____ **18.** Which animals have alveoli?

    a. fish   c. mammals

    b. amphibians   d. all chordates

_____ **19.** The circulatory systems of gilled vertebrates have

    a. a single loop.   c. a single chamber.

    b. a double loop.   d. three chambers.

_____ **20.** The vertebrate brain is

    a. a mass of nerve cells.

    b. complex with distinct regions.

    c. not specialized for complex behavior.

    d. located at the posterior end of the spinal cord.

Chapter 33 Comparing Chordates · Enrichment

Burgess Shale Fossils

One of the earliest known chordates, *Pikaia,* was found in Canada's Rocky Mountains in a fossil deposit known as the Burgess Shale, in the Province of British Columbia. The Burgess Shale is a unique rock formation because it contains countless fossils of soft-bodied organisms. Most fossils that are found today are of organisms whose bodies included hard parts, such as shells or bones. When the organisms died, the soft tissues usually decomposed, leaving only the hard skeletons to become mineralized over time as fossils.

The soft-bodied fossils of the Burgess Shale were once marine animals that lived near a huge undersea reef in a warm ocean. Occasional mudslides would wash animals over the edge of the reef hundreds of feet to the deep ocean floor. Once there, low oxygen levels protected the animals from scavengers and decomposition. They were also covered with a very fine clay mud. The clay particles infiltrated every body tissue, preserving the entire animal, including internal organs, as a fossil.

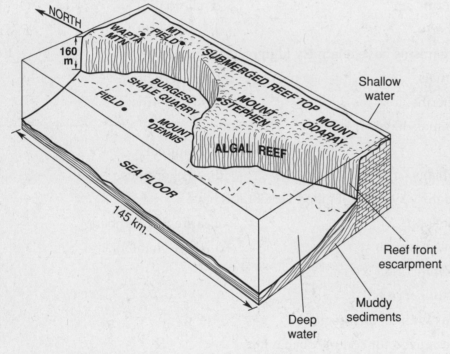

This is what the Burgess Shale deposit may have looked like 500 million years ago when it was formed at the edge of an ocean reef. The diagram also identifies mountains, such as Mount Odaray, that exist today.

In the 500 million years since these animals were buried, the tectonic forces that built the Rocky Mountains lifted the reef and mud deposits out of the ocean. During these many years, the mud deposits were transformed into the Burgess Shale. Weathering of the shale causes it to break off, exposing the fossils. Scientists have also quarried the shale to expose even more of the hidden fossil treasures.

Evaluation *Answer the following questions on a separate sheet of paper.*

1. Based on the article, explain the main requirement for a soft-bodied animal to become fossilized.

2. Sedimentary rock is formed from deposits of sediment over long periods of time. Based on this definition, explain whether the Burgess Shale is a sedimentary rock.

Chapter 33 Comparing Chordates   **Graphic Organizer**

Flowchart

Complete the flowchart below to show the sequence in which important adaptations appeared during the course of chordate evolution.

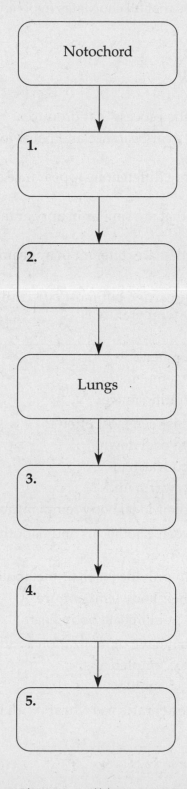

Notochord

1.

2.

Lungs

3.

4.

5.

Chapter 33 Comparing Chordates   **Chapter Test A**

Multiple Choice

Write the letter that best answers the question or completes the statement on the line provided.

_____ 1. A phylogenetic tree shows that all chordates evolved from
   a. tunicates and lancelets.
   b. dinosaur ancestors.
   c. fishes.
   d. a common ancestor.

_____ 2. Convergent evolution is the process that produces
   a. species that are similar in appearance and behavior but not closely related.
   b. unrelated species that are different in appearance and behavior.
   c. closely related species that are similar in appearance and behavior.
   d. closely related species that are different in appearance and behavior.

_____ 3. Essential life functions are carried out most efficiently when an animal's internal body temperature is
   a. insulated.
   b. regulated by the environment.
   c. the same as its external temperature.
   d. within a particular operating range.

_____ 4. Panting is a behavior that is seen most often in
   a. endotherms that need to cool down.
   b. endotherms that need to warm up.
   c. ectotherms that need to warm up.
   d. ectotherms that are at their ideal body temperature.

_____ 5. The main difference between ectotherms and endotherms is
   a. the source of their body heat.
   b. how they obtain food to provide for their metabolism.
   c. whether they control their body temperature.
   d. whether they conserve or eliminate body heat.

_____ 6. The simplest chordates that have cephalization as adults are
   a. lancelets.   c. amphibians.
   b. fishes.   d. reptiles.

_____ 7. Which of the following vertebrates has a heart with four chambers?
   a. a salamander   c. a goldfish
   b. a lizard   d. a cow

_____ **8.** Chordate respiratory structures include all of the following EXCEPT

    a. simple air sacs.

    b. the medulla oblongata.

    c. the surface of the skin.

    d. the lining of the mouth.

_____ **9.** When a fish respires, water flows in which of the following patterns?

    a. in through the gill slits, over the gill filaments, and out through the mouth

    b. in through the gill filaments, over the gill slits, and out through the mouth

    c. in through the mouth, over the gill slits, and out through the gill filaments

    d. in through the mouth, over the gill filaments, and out through the gill slits

_____ **10.** The main difference between an amphibian lung and a reptilian lung is that

    a. an amphibian lung has a greater surface for gas exchange.

    b. a reptilian lung has a greater surface area for gas exchange.

    c. an amphibian lung contains thousands of alveoli, but a reptilian lung does not.

    d. a reptilian lung is connected to air sacs, but an amphibian lung is not.

_____ **11.** In a single-loop circulatory system, the atrium

    a. receives the blood from the body.

    b. pumps blood to the gills.

    c. pumps blood to the lungs.

    d. pumps blood throughout the entire body.

_____ **12.** A single-loop circulatory system is characteristic of

    a. fishes.

    b. adult amphibians.

    c. most reptiles.

    d. crocodilians.

_____ **13.** A function of ligaments in a backbone is to

    a. generate forward thrust during swimming.

    b. keep the backbone straight and rigid.

    c. connect the vertebrae.

    d. make the body bend back and forth.

_____ **14.** The sets of bones that support the limbs of vertebrates are called

    a. vertebral columns.   c. ligaments.

    b. limb girdles.   d. vertebrae.

_____**15.** Embryos obtain nutrients from the yolk inside the egg in
   a. oviparous and ovoviviparous animals.
   b. viviparous and ovoviviparous animals.
   c. viviparous and oviparous animals.
   d. viviparous animals only.

Completion

Complete each statement on the line provided.

16. Over the course of evolution, the appearance of new adaptations has launched _____ in chordate groups.

17. A(An) _____ is an animal whose body temperature is controlled mainly by the transfer of heat between its body and its surroundings.

18. An animal that strains small pieces of food from the water is called a(an) _____ .

19. In mammalian lungs, _____ provide an enormous surface area for gas exchange.

20. The region of your brain that you use to determine the answers to test questions is called the _____ .

Short Answer

In complete sentences, write the answers to the questions on the lines provided.

21. If two extinct but unrelated species of chordates shared many adaptations, what can you infer about the ecological conditions those species encountered?

_____

_____

22. Animals A and B are terrestrial vertebrates of the same size. One is an ectotherm and the other is an endotherm. The resting metabolic rate of animal A is five times that of animal B. Using this information, state which animal is the ectotherm and briefly explain your conclusion.

_____

_____

23. Are the simple organ systems of a tunicate inferior to the organ systems of a mammal?

_____

_____

24. In what ways other than length do the digestive tracts of carnivores and herbivores differ?

_____

_____

Name______________________ Class______________ Date ____________

25. Contrast movement in larval and adult tunicates.

____

____

Using Science Skills

Use the diagram below to answer the following questions on the lines provided.

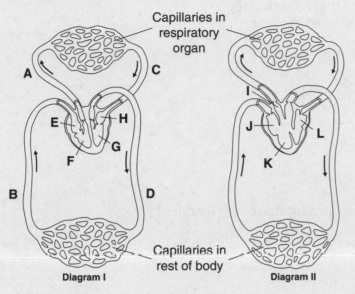

Capillaries in
respiratory
organ
A
C
I
E
H
J
L
G
F
K
B
D
Capillaries in
rest of body
Diagram I
Diagram II

Figure 1

26. **Interpreting Graphics** Figure 1 shows two types of vertebrate circulatory systems. In Diagram I, which of the vessels labeled A, B, C, and D contain(s) oxygen-rich blood, and which contain(s) oxygen-poor blood?

____

____

____

27. **Interpreting Graphics** Name the four heart chambers (labeled E, F, G, and H) in Diagram I.

____

____

____

28. **Interpreting Graphics** In Diagram II, where does blood go after it leaves the chamber labeled K?

____

____

____

29. **Applying Concepts** Which group(s) of vertebrates—fishes, crocodilians, noncrocodilian reptiles, birds, mammals—have a circulatory system that is represented by each diagram in Figure 1?

_____

_____

_____

30. **Comparing and Contrasting** Describe the main difference between the two circulatory systems shown in Figure 1.

_____

_____

_____

_____

Essay

Write the answer to each question in the space provided.

31. Why is the control of body temperature important for vertebrates?

32. Describe two hypotheses concerning the evolution of endothermy in vertebrates. What does the evidence on this issue suggest?

33. Contrast the respiratory systems of mammals and birds.

34. Describe the major differences among the chambers of the heart in the five main groups of vertebrates.

35. Describe the forms in which nitrogenous wastes are eliminated in different groups of chordates.

Chapter 33 Comparing Chordates — Chapter Test B

Multiple Choice

Write the letter that best answers the question or completes the statement on the line provided.

_____ 1. *Pikaia* was an early
   a. worm.
   b. vertebrate.
   c. chordate.

_____ 2. Which of the following is NOT an adaptation that appeared during the course of chordate evolution?
   a. endothermy
   b. radial symmetry
   c. four limbs

_____ 3. The notochord is a characteristic of
   a. worms.
   b. all chordates.
   c. mammals only.

_____ 4. The rapid growth in the diversity of a group of organisms is called
   a. a ladogram.
   b. adaptive radiation.
   c. convergent radiation.

_____ 5. The largest living group of chordates is the
   a. amphibians.
   b. fishes.
   c. mammals.

_____ 6. Which of the following animals is an ectotherm?
   a. bluebird
   b. snake
   c. squirrel

_____ 7. Which of the following help mammals retain body heat?
   a. hair and sweat glands
   b. hair and body fat
   c. bones and sweat glands

_____ 8. Filter feeders include all of the following EXCEPT
   a. lancelets.
   b. flamingos.
   c. crocodiles.

_____ 9. Colonies of bacteria in the intestines of a cow are helpful in
   a. digesting cellulose fibers.
   b. producing enzymes that digest meat.
   c. straining plankton from water.

_____10. What is the general rule regarding respiratory organs in chordates?
    a. Aquatic chordates use lungs, and land vertebrates use gills.
    b. Aquatic chordates use lungs and gills, and land vertebrates use gills.
    c. Aquatic chordates use gills, and land vertebrates use lungs.

_____11. The most efficient vertebrate lungs are found in
    a. amphibians.
    b. reptiles.
    c. birds.

_____12. The heart of a fish has
    a. one atrium and one ventricle.
    b. one atrium and two ventricles.
    c. two atria and one ventricle.

_____13. In tunicates, some nitrogenous wastes leave the body in the form of
    a. urea.
    b. ammonia.
    c. uric acid.

_____14. Which of the following characteristic(s) is(are) shared by all chordates?
    a. a bony skeleton
    b. pharyngeal pouches
    c. a backbone

_____15. Internal fertilization occurs in
    a. fishes.
    b. amphibians.
    c. mammals.

Completion

Complete each statement on the line provided.

16. The chordate family tree has its roots in ancestors that vertebrates share with tunicates and _____ .

17. In environments where temperatures are high and fairly constant most of the time, _____ is a more energy-efficient method of controlling body temperature.

18. In a mammalian lung, gas exchange occurs inside bubblelike structures called _____ .

19. If an animal has a four-chambered heart, it has a _____ -loop circulatory system.

20. Animals whose embryos obtain nutrition directly from the mother's body are said to have _____ development.

Short Answer

In complete sentences, write the answers to the questions on the lines provided.

21. Identify four features common to all chordates.

_____

_____

_____

_____

22. List three features that are included in the ways in which all vertebrates control their body temperature.

_____

_____

_____

23. Describe the basic pathways of the two loops in a double-loop circulatory system.

_____

_____

_____

24. List two functions of vertebrate kidneys.

_____

_____

_____

25. Describe the functions of the optic lobes and olfactory bulbs in a vertebrate brain.

_____

_____

_____

Using Science Skills

Use the diagram below to answer the following questions on the lines provided.

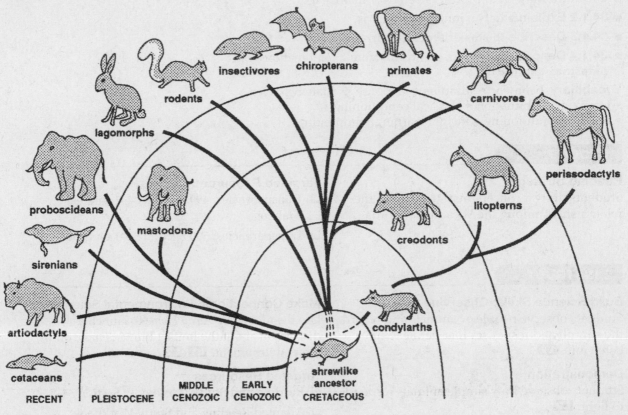

Figure 1

26. **Interpreting Graphics** According to Figure 1, which extinct group of mammals descended from the condylarths?

   _____

27. **Interpreting Graphics** According to Figure 1, during which era, period, or epoch did the ancestors of the creodonts and the carnivores split into two different lines?

   _____

28. **Interpreting Graphics** Use Figure 1 to identify two groups of mammals that are extinct.

   _____

29. **Classifying** According to Figure 1, to which living order of mammals are sirenians most closely related?

   _____

30. **Classifying** According to Figure 1, are insectivores more closely related to rodents or to chiropterans?

   _____

LESSON PLAN 34–1 (pages 871–876)

Elements of Behavior

Section Objectives

- **34.1.1 Identify** what produces behavior in animals.
- **34.1.2 Explain** what an innate behavior is.
- **34.1.3 Describe** the major types of learning.
- **34.1.4 Describe** behaviors that result from a combination of instinct and learning.

Vocabulary behavior • stimulus • response • innate behavior • learning • habituation • classical conditioning • operant conditioning • insight learning • imprinting

Local Standards

1 FOCUS

Reading Strategy
Students draw a concept map that shows the relationships among the Vocabulary words.

Targeted Resources
- ❏ Transparencies: **499** Section 34–1 Interest Grabber
- ❏ Transparencies: **500** Section 34–1 Outline

2 INSTRUCT

Build Science Skills: Observing
Students observe people or animals and record the stimuli and responses that define their behaviors. **L2**

Demonstration
Students observe how simple animals respond to light. **L2**

Build Science Skills: Applying Concepts
Students observe a simple innate behavior in humans. **L2**

Build Science Skills: Using Analogies
Students apply the concept of habituation to Aesop's fable about the boy who cried wolf. **L2 L3**

Use Visuals: Figure 34–5
Use Figure 34–5 to review classical conditioning. **L1 L2**

Make Connections: Environmental Science
Use the movie *Fly Away Home* to launch a discussion about the impact humans have on their environment. **L1 L2**

Targeted Resources
- ❏ Reading and Study Workbook: Section 34–1
- ❏ Adapted Reading and Study Workbook: Section 34–1
- ❏ Teaching Resources: Section Summaries 34–1, Worksheets 34–1
- ❏ Transparencies: **501** Inheritance of Wing-Flipping Behavior in Moths, **502** Figure 34–5 Pavlov's Experiment
- ❏ Lab Manual A: Chapter 34 Lab
- ❏ Lab Manual B: Chapter 34 Lab

3 ASSESS

Evaluate Understanding
Orally quiz students about behavior and learning.

Reteach
Students identify the type of behavior exemplified by each figure in the section.

Targeted Resources
- ❏ Teaching Resources: Section Review 34–1
- ❏ *i Text* Section 34–1

LESSON PLAN 34–2 (pages 878–882)

Patterns of Behavior

Time
2 periods
1 block

Section Objectives

Local Standards

- **34.2.1 Explain** how environmental changes affect animal behavior.
- **34.2.2 Describe** how courtship and social behavior increase an animal's evolutionary fitness.
- **34.2.3 Identify** behavioral patterns used to claim and defend territories.
- **34.2.4 Summarize** how animals communicate.

Vocabulary migration • circadian rhythm • courtship • territory • aggression • communication • language

1 FOCUS

Vocabulary Preview
Break down the word *circadian* into its word parts to help with meaning.

Targeted Resources
- ❏ Transparencies: **503** Section 34–2 Interest Grabber
- ❏ Transparencies: **504** Section 34–2 Outline
- ❏ Transparencies: **505** Concept Map

2 INSTRUCT

Use Visuals: Figure 34–8
Use Figure 34–8 to reinforce the behavioral cycle of migration. **L1** **L2**

Build Science Skills: Applying Concepts
Students learn about courtship behaviors of different animals. **L2** **L3**

Build Science Skills: Formulating Hypotheses
Students hypothesize about how the amount of danger animals face affects their aggressiveness. **L2**

Demonstration
Communicate to the class without using language. **L2**

Make Connections: Chemistry
Discuss the chemistry of pheromones and how they affect behavior. **L2**

Targeted Resources
- ❏ Reading and Study Workbook: Section 34–2
- ❏ Adapted Reading and Study Workbook: Section 34–2
- ❏ Transparencies: **506** Figure 34–8 Migration of Sea Turtles
- ❏ Teaching Resources: Section Summaries: 34–2, Worksheets 34–2, Enrichment
- ❏ Lab Worksheets: Chapter 34 Design an Experiment
- ❏ **NSTA** *sci*LINKS Animal communication

3 ASSESS

Evaluate Understanding
Students write a paragraph about animal communication.

Reteach
Student pairs develop a graphic organizer that shows the relationships of the Vocabulary words.

Targeted Resources
- ❏ Teaching Resources: Section Review 34–2, Chapter Vocabulary Review, Graphic Organizer, Chapter 34 Tests: Levels A and B
- ❏ Lab Assessment: Laboratory Assessment 9
- ❏ 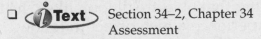 Section 34–2, Chapter 34 Assessment
- ❏ **PHSchool.com** Online Chapter 34 Test

Chapter 34   Animal Behavior

Summary

34–1 Elements of Behavior

Behavior is the way that an organism reacts to change. The change may be within the body or in the environment. Most behavior takes place when an animal reacts to a **stimulus**. A **response** is a reaction to a stimulus. Animals detect stimuli with their sense organs. **When an animal responds to a stimulus, different body systems interact to produce the resultant behavior.**

Innate behaviors are fully functional the first time they are performed, even though the animal may have had no previous experience with the stimuli to which it responds. Examples of innate behaviors are the suckling of a newborn mammal and the weaving of a spider web.

Learning is the way that animals change their behavior as a result of experience. **Animals learn in four major ways:**

- **Habituation** is the simplest form of learning. In habituation, an animal's response to a stimulus slows or stops when the animal is neither rewarded nor harmed for responding. For example, ragworms will retreat into their burrows if a shadow passes overhead. However, when repeated shadows pass overhead, they will stop retreating to their burrows.
- **Classical conditioning** occurs when a mental connection between a stimulus and an event is made. Ivan Pavlov rang a bell each time he fed his dog. Eventually, he found that the dog would start salivating whenever the bell rang, whether or not food was presented.
- In **operant conditioning,** an animal learns to act in a certain way to get a reward or to avoid punishment. Operant conditioning is known as trial-and-error learning. It begins when a random behavior is rewarded.
- **Insight learning** is the most complex form of learning. In insight learning, an animal applies something already learned to a new situation. Insight learning occurs mostly in humans.

Most behaviors are the result of both innate behavior and learning. An example is **imprinting.** Newborn ducks and geese have an innate urge to follow the first moving object they see. Usually, this object is their parent. They are not born knowing what that object will look like. The newborn must learn from experience which object to follow.

34–2 Patterns of Behavior

Animal behaviors may occur in patterns. **Many animals respond to periodic changes in the environment with daily or seasonal cycles of behavior.** Dormancy, migration, and circadian rhythms are examples. **Circadian rhythms** occur in a daily pattern, such as sleeping at night and going to school during the day.

Behaviors can help animals reproduce. **Courtship behavior is part of an overall reproductive strategy that helps many animals identify healthy mates.** Some courtship behaviors include elaborate rituals. Most rituals have specific signals and responses.

Animals exhibit social behavior when they interact with members of their own species. Many animals form societies. A society is a group of related animals of the same species that interact closely and often cooperate with one another. Being a part of an animal society helps improve an individual's evolutionary fitness. Termites form societies. So do zebras, wild dogs, and primates. Animal societies use "strength in numbers" to better hunt, protect territory, guard young, and fight rivals.

Some animal behaviors keep other animals from using limited resources. These resources may be food, water, or shelter. Such behaviors help protect territories. A **territory** is the area lived in and protected by an animal or group of animals.

Territories have resources that an animal needs to survive and reproduce. Competition occurs when two or more animals claim the same territory. During competition, one animal may use aggression to gain control over another. **Aggression** is threatening behavior.

Communication is the passing of information from one animal to another. **Animals communicate in many ways.**

- Animals with good eyesight may communicate with visual signals. These signals may include movement and color.
- Animals with a well-developed sense of smell communicate with chemicals called **pheromones.** The chemicals affect the behavior of other members of the species. For example, some animals use pheromones to mark territory.
- Animals with strong vocal abilities communicate with sound. Birds, toads, crickets, and dolphins use sound to communicate.
- **Language** is the most complex form of communication. Language combines sounds, symbols, and gestures according to sets of rules about word order and meaning. Only humans are known to use language.

Stimulus and Response

A stimulus is any signal that carries information and can be detected. A response is a specific reaction to a stimulus.

Use the information in the diagrams to answer the questions.

Stimulus: ___Presence of food___

Response: _____

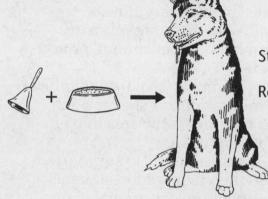

Stimulus: _____

Response: _____

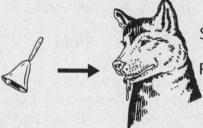

Stimulus: _____

Response: _____

1. Describe the experiment shown in the diagrams.

_____

_____

_____

_____

2. What type of learning is shown in this experiment?

_____

Innate and Learned Behaviors

An innate behavior is one that is fully functional the first time an animal uses it, even though the animal has no experience with the stimulus that causes it. These behaviors are inborn. Other behaviors are acquired through experience. These are called learned behaviors.

Identify each behavior as innate *or* learned. *Two examples have been completed for you.*

Behavior	Innate or Learned
spider spinning a web	innate
child riding a bicycle	learned
baby crying	
newborn mammal suckling	
birds conditioned to push a lever	
baby birds recognizing their species' song	
baboons washing sweet potatoes	

Answer the question.

1. What is another example of a learned behavior?

_____

_____

Types of Learned Behaviors

Animals learn behaviors in four primary ways. Most of these ways of learning involve making a connection between a behavior and a reward or punishment.

Use the words below to complete the table.

classical conditioning	insight learning
habituation	operant conditioning

Type of Learning	How It Works	Example
	An animal makes a mental connection between a stimulus and a reward or punishment.	Pavlov's dog learned that the sound of a bell was associated with food, so it salivated at the sound.
	An animal stops responding to a stimulus that brings neither reward nor punishment.	A shore ragworm stops responding if shadows pass over it repeatedly.
	An animal learns through trial and error to behave in a certain way to get a reward or to avoid punishment.	A pigeon learns that if it presses a button, it will receive food.
	An animal applies something it has already learned to a new situation, without a trial-and-error period.	A chimpanzee stacks boxes to reach high-hanging bananas.

Use the table to answer the question. Circle the best answer.

1. Which is the most complicated type of learning?

    habituation   insight learning

Behavioral Cycles

Many animal behaviors are related to changes in the environment. Environmental cycles, such as the sequence of day and night or the passing of seasons, can lead to cycles in animal behavior.

Use the words below to identify each behavioral cycle.

circadian rhythms	dormancy	migration

Behavior	Description	Example
	Animals periodically move from one place to another and then back again.	Birds fly south for the winter.
	Behavioral cycles that occur in daily patterns	People naturally sleep at night and are awake during the day.
	Animals are active during warm seasons and enter a sleeplike state during cold seasons.	Some reptiles hibernate through the winter.

Use the table to answer the question.

1. Why is dormancy useful to some animals?

_____

_____

2. Why do animals usually migrate?

_____

_____

Communication

Bees can communicate the distance and location of food through their dances. In the "waggle dance," a bee runs in a straight line, waggling its abdomen. It then circles back, runs straight again, and circles back the other way. The distance it runs before circling tells other bees how far away the food is. The longer the bee runs and the more it waggles, the farther away the food. The direction of the dance also indicates the location of the food.

The solid arrows show how long the bee's straight path is.

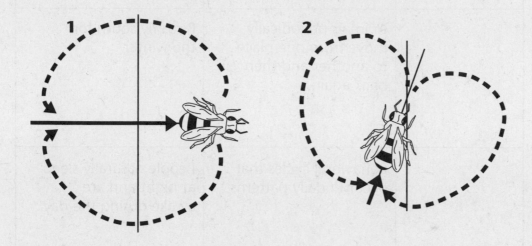

Use the diagrams to answer the question.

1. If a bee wanted to find a food source nearby, which bee would it be most likely to follow?

   _____

2. Draw a diagram showing another "waggle dance." The food source for your dance is the same distance away as the food source shown by bee 1. However, the new food source is located in the opposite direction as the source shown by bee 1.

Courtship Behavior

Animals use many behaviors to find and attract mates. Successful courtship behaviors help animals identify healthy mates. For many birds, songs are courtship behaviors. The graph shows the relationship between the number of songs that the males of a particular species of warbler know and the length of time it takes the birds to find a mate.

On the graph, draw a straight line that best fits the data.

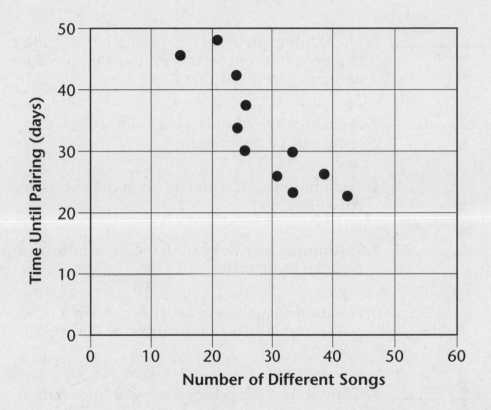

Use the graph to answer the questions.

1. Describe the relationship between the number of songs that a male warbler knows and the time until it pairs with a mate.

   _____

   _____

2. How could the number of songs that a male warbler knows affect its chances for reproductive success?

   _____

   _____

Chapter 34   Animal Behavior

Vocabulary Review

True or False   *If the statement is true, write* true. *If it is false, write* false.

_____ 1. Learning based on early experience, such as geese learning to follow the first moving object they see during a certain time early in their lives, is called migration.

_____ 2. Habituation involves decreasing or stopping a response to a repetitive stimulus that provides neither reward nor harm.

_____ 3. A circadian rhythm is a behavioral cycle that occurs in a daily pattern.

_____ 4. Trial-and-error learning is often called classical conditioning.

_____ 5. A stimulus is any signal that carries information and can be detected.

_____ 6. An animal engages in courtship when it sends out stimuli to attract a member of the opposite sex.

_____ 7. Communication is the passing of information from one organism to another.

_____ 8. Insight learning behaviors are those an animal is born knowing how to exhibit.

_____ 9. A stimulus is a single, specific reaction to a stimulus.

_____ 10. Imprinting is the way an organism reacts to changes in its internal condition or external environment.

Summary

34–1 Elements of Behavior

Behavior is the way an organism reacts to changes within its body or in its environment. Behaviors usually occur when an animal reacts to a stimulus. The single, specific reaction to a stimulus is a response. Animals detect stimuli with their sense organs. When an animal responds, the nervous system and the muscles work together to produce the behavior.

Animal behavior is important to survival and reproduction. Some behaviors are controlled by genes. They are influenced by natural selection. Organisms with a certain behavior may survive and reproduce better than organisms without the behavior. Over time, most individuals in the population will have that behavior.

Some behaviors are innate. These behaviors are fully functional the first time they are performed, even though the animal may have had no previous experience with the stimuli to which it responds. Examples of innate behaviors are the suckling of a newborn mammal and the weaving of a spider web.

Learning is the way animals change their behavior as a result of experience. Acquired behavior is another name for learning, because these behaviors develop over time. Animals learn in different ways. These include habituation, classical conditioning, operant conditioning, and insight learning.

Habituation is the simplest way in which animals learn. In habituation, an animal's response to a stimulus decreases or stops when the animal is neither rewarded nor harmed for responding.

Classical conditioning occurs when an animal makes a mental connection between a stimulus and a good or bad event. One famous example was described by Ivan Pavlov. Pavlov discovered that if he rang a bell when he fed his dog, the dog would begin to salivate whenever he rang the bell.

In operant conditioning, an animal learns to behave in a certain way in order to receive a reward or to avoid punishment. Operant conditioning is also called trial-and-error learning because it begins with a random behavior that is rewarded.

Insight learning, or reasoning, is the most complicated form of learning. In insight learning, an animal applies something it has already learned to a new situation. Insight learning is found most often in humans.

Most behaviors are the result of innate behavior and learning combined. One example of this is imprinting. Newborn ducks and geese have an innate urge to follow the first moving object they see. They are not born knowing what that object will look like. The newborn must learn from experience what object to follow.

34–2 Patterns of Behavior

Many animal behaviors occur in patterns. These patterns often follow the natural cycles of day and night, seasonal changes, or moon phases. Examples of cycles of behavior include dormancy, migration, and circadian rhythms. Dormancy allows an animal to survive periods when food and other resources may not be available. Migration is the periodic movement from one place to another and then back again. Circadian rhythms occur in a daily pattern, like sleeping at night and going to school during the day.

Animal behaviors also help animals reproduce. Courtship behaviors help an animal find a healthy mate. Some courtship behaviors involve an elaborate series of rituals. Most rituals have specific signals and responses.

Animals have social behavior whenever they interact with members of their own species. Many animals form societies. A society is a group of related animals of the same species that interact closely and often cooperate with one another. Termites form societies. So do zebras, wild dogs, and primates. Animal societies use their strength in numbers to improve their ability to hunt, protect their territory, guard their young, and fight rivals.

Some animal behaviors help prevent others from using limited resources. These behaviors help protect territories. A territory is the area occupied and protected by an animal or group of animals. Territories contain resources, such as food, water, and shelter, that an animal needs to survive and reproduce.

Competition occurs when two or more animals claim the same territory. During competition, an animal may use threatening behavior, or aggression, to gain control over the other animal.

Communication is the passing of information from one animal to another. Animals use many different ways to communicate. Animals with good eyesight often use visual signals such as movement and color to communicate.

Animals with a well-developed sense of smell produce chemicals called pheromones. These chemicals affect the behavior of other members of the species, to mark a territory, for example.

Animals with strong vocal abilities communicate with sound. Birds, toads, crickets, and dolphins use sound to communicate.

Language is the most complicated form of communication. Language combines sounds, symbols, and gestures according to sets of rules about word order and meaning. Only humans are known to use language.

Chapter 34 Animal Behavior

Section 34–1 Elements of Behavior (pages 871–876)

🔑 **Key Concepts**
- What produces behavior in animals?
- What is an innate behavior?
- What are the major types of learning?

Stimulus and Response (pages 871–872)

1. How do biologists define behavior? _____
_____
_____

2. Behaviors are usually performed when an animal reacts to a(an) _____.

3. What is a response? _____
_____

4. Circle the letter of each response.
   a. alarm ringing
   c. answering the phone
   b. hunger pangs
   d. swimming toward moving prey

5. Circle the letter of each stimulus.
   a. light
   c. heat
   b. sound
   d. odors

6. Is the following sentence true or false? All animals can detect all types of stimuli.
   _____

7. What body systems interact to produce a behavior in response to a stimulus?
_____
_____

8. Is the following sentence true or false? Animals with more complex nervous systems can respond to stimuli with more complicated and precise behaviors. _____

Behavior and Evolution (page 872)

9. Is the following sentence true or false? Animal behaviors are not influenced by genes.
   _____

10. Explain how natural selection works in the evolution of behaviors in a population.
_____
_____
_____
_____

Innate Behavior (page 873)

11. What is an innate behavior? _____

_____

_____

_____

12. What two things interact to cause innate behaviors?

    a. _____

    b. _____

Learned Behavior (pages 873–875)

13. What is learning? _____

_____

14. List the four major types of learning.

    a. _____   c. _____

    b. _____   d. _____

15. The process by which an animal decreases or stops its response to a repetitive stimulus that neither rewards nor harms the animal is called _____.

16. What is the advantage of habituation? _____

_____

_____

17. Identify the type of learning illustrated below. _____
    What is the stimulus? _____ What is the reward or
    punishment that is associated with the stimulus? _____

18. What is operant conditioning? _____
_____
_____

19. How does a Skinner box work in operant conditioning? _____
_____
_____
_____

20. When does insight learning occur? _____
_____
_____

21. Is the following sentence true or false? Insight learning is common among reptiles and amphibians. _____

Instinct and Learning Combined (page 876)

22. What is the purpose of imprinting? _____
_____
_____

23. Is the following sentence true or false? Imprinting can be changed after it has occurred.
_____

Reading Skill Practice

When you read a section, taking notes can help you organize and remember the information. As you read or review Section 34–1, take notes by writing each heading and listing the main points under each heading. Do your work on a separate sheet of paper.

Section 34–2 Patterns of Behavior (pages 878–882)

⟳ **Key Concepts**
- How do environmental changes affect animal behavior?
- How do courtship and social behaviors increase an animal's evolutionary fitness?
- How do animals communicate?

Behavioral Cycles (page 878)

Match the behavioral cycle with its description.

Behavioral Cycle	Description
_____ 1. Dormancy _____ 2. Migration _____ 3. Circadian rhythms	**a.** A sleeplike state that allows an animal to survive periods when food or other resources may not be available **b.** Behavioral cycles that occur in daily patterns, such as sleeping at night and attending school during the day **c.** The periodic movement from one place to another and then back again to take advantage of favorable environmental conditions

Courtship (page 879)

4. Circle the letter of each sentence that is true about courtship.

   a. Courtship behavior helps animals identify healthy mates.

   b. In courtship, an individual sends out stimuli to attract a member of the opposite sex.

   c. Fireflies have an elaborate dance to indicate their readiness to mate.

   d. Courtship rituals always involve a single behavior.

Social Behavior (page 880)

5. Is the following sentence true or false? Courtship is an example of a social behavior.

   _____

6. A group of related animals of the same species that interact closely and often cooperate with one another is called a(an) _____ .

7. What are the advantages of animal societies? _____

   _____

   _____

8. How does helping a relative survive improve an individual's evolutionary fitness?

   _____

   _____

   _____

   _____

Competition and Aggression (page 881)

9. What is a territory? _____

_____

_____

10. Circle the letter of each resource that animals need to survive and reproduce.

    a. odors   **c.** nesting sites

    b. mates   **d.** water

11. When does competition occur? _____

_____

_____

12. A threatening behavior that one animal uses to gain control over another is

_____.

Communication (pages 881–882)

13. What is communication? _____

_____

14. Is the following sentence true or false? Animals with poor eyesight often use visual signals involving movement and color. _____

15. Some animals communicate using _____, chemical messengers that affect the behavior of other individuals of the same species.

16. Is the following sentence true or false? Some animals that use sound to communicate, such as dolphins, might live in places where vision is not very useful. _____

Vocabulary Review

Completion   *Fill in the blanks with terms from Chapter 34.*

1. The way an animal reacts to changes within itself or its environment is called

    _____.

2. A single, specific reaction to a stimulus is a(an) _____.

3. Animals that change their behavior as a result of experience are

    _____.

4. In _____ conditioning, an animal learns to make a mental connection between a stimulus and a reward or punishment.

5. A behavioral cycle that occurs in a daily pattern is a(an) _____.

6. A specific area that is occupied and protected by an animal is its

    _____.

7. The passing of information from one organism to another is called

    _____.

8. The system of communication that only humans are known to use is

    _____.

True or False   *In the space, write* true *if the statement is true. If the statement is false, write the term that makes the statement true.*

_____ 9. A <u>stimulus</u> is any kind of signal that carries information and can be detected.

_____ 10. An <u>innate behavior</u> is an instinct.

_____ 11. <u>Insight learning</u> occurs when an animal stops its response to a repetitive stimulus that is harmless.

_____ 12. Ducklings exhibit <u>operant conditioning</u> when they follow the first moving object they see.

_____ 13. <u>Migration</u> is the periodic movement from one place to another and back again.

_____ 14. In <u>learning</u>, an individual sends out stimuli in order to attract a member of the opposite sex.

_____ 15. <u>Aggression</u> is a threatening behavior that one animal uses to gain control over another.

Chapter 34 Animal Behavior   Section Review 34-1

Reviewing Key Concepts

Completion *On the lines provided, complete the following sentences.*

1. A _____ is a way an organism reacts to changes in its internal condition or external environment.

2. A _____ is any kind of signal that carries information and can be detected.

3. When an animal responds to a stimulus, _____ interact with sense organs and the nervous system to produce a behavior.

4. Information is passed along nerve cells to the _____, which processes the information and directs a response.

Short Answer *On the lines provided, answer the following question:*

5. Define innate behavior, and give an example of this type of behavior.

_____

_____

Completion *In the boxes provided, complete the table about the four different types of learning.*

Type of Learning	Description	Example
6.	An animal decreases its response to a stimulus that neither rewards nor harms it.	A ragworm learns to ignore a shadow passing overhead.
Classical Conditioning	7.	Pavlov's dogs were conditioned to salivate when they heard a bell ring.
8.	An animal learns to behave in a certain way through repeated practice.	After several trials, an animal learns to press a lever to get food.
Insight Learning	An animal applies something it has already learned to a new situation.	9.

Reviewing Key Skills

10. **Applying Concepts** Suppose a dog becomes frightened every time it rides in a car. How might you train the dog not to be afraid?

_____

_____

_____

Reviewing Key Concepts

Completion *On the lines provided, complete the following sentences.*

1. Daily or seasonal cycles of behavior usually occur in response to periodic changes in the _____.

2. Seasonal movement from one location to another and back again is called _____.

3. Behavioral cycles that occur in daily patterns are called _____.

4. The behavior that helps animals identify and attract a healthy mate is called _____.

5. A(an) _____ is made up of animals of the same species that work together to benefit the group.

6. _____ involves the passing of information from one organism to another, in the form of visual, chemical, touch, or sound signals.

Short Answer *On the lines provided, answer the following questions:*

7. What is aggression? Describe an example.

_____

_____

8. How does cooperation among animals in a society promote the evolutionary success of individual animals? Explain your answer.

_____

_____

_____

Reviewing Key Skills

9. **Comparing and Contrasting** How is a city or town similar to an animal society? How is it different from an animal society?

_____

_____

_____

_____

10. **Applying Concepts** Describe one way in which you respond to seasonal changes in your environment.

_____

_____

_____

Chapter 34 Animal Behavior   Chapter Vocabulary Review

Crosswood Puzzle

Use the clues below and on the following page to complete the puzzle.

Across

1. the process in which a young animal learns to recognize and follow the first moving object it sees

3. the alteration of behavior as a result of experience

5. occurs when an animal learns to ignore a nonthreatening or unrewarding stimulus

6. any kind of signal that carries information and can be detected

8. a single, specific reaction to a stimulus

11. type of conditioning studied by Pavlov

12. a specific area that is occupied and protected by an animal or group of animals

13. the passing of information from one organism to another

14. type of learning that occurs when an animal applies something it has already learned to a new situation (reasoning)

Down

1. type of behavior that is also called instinct or inborn behavior

2. the way an organism reacts to changes in its internal condition or external environment

4. system of communication that carries complex messages

7. type of conditioning that is also called trial-and-error learning

9. seasonal movement from one area to another and then back again

10. behavioral cycle that occurs in daily patterns: a circadian _____.

Multiple Choice *On the lines provided, write the letter of the answer that best answers the question or completes the sentence.*

_____ 15. Pavlov's experiment, in which dogs learned to associate a ringing bell with food, is an example of
   a. classical conditioning.   c. habituation.
   b. operant conditioning.   d. insight learning.

_____ 16. Sleeping at night and going to school during the day is an example of
   a. a courtship.   c. habituation.
   b. a circadian rhythm.   d. a migration.

_____ 17. An individual sends out stimuli in order to attract a member of the opposite sex during
   a. habituation.   c. courtship.
   b. migration.   d. aggression.

_____ 18. The area that contains the resources an animal needs to survive is called a
   a. territory.   c. society.
   b. hunting ground.   d. mating space.

_____ 19. When an animal uses threatening behavior to gain control over another animal, it is showing
   a. imprinting.   c. aggression.
   b. conditioning.   d. migration.

_____ 20. The kind of communication exhibited only by humans is
   a. chemical signals.   c. visual cues.
   b. sound signals.   d. language.

Chapter 34 Animal Behavior

Hibernation

In winter some birds migrate to places with warmer weather. Other animals grow thicker coats to keep themselves warm or change color to blend in with their surroundings, like snowshoe hares. Animals such as ground squirrels and woodchucks, who have little to eat during the winter months, may enter a physically dormant state called hibernation.

Hibernation allows the animal to maintain the body functions necessary for survival while conserving energy by lowering its body temperature. Scientists do not know how animals sense when to hibernate. Hibernating animals seem to have an annual clock that is synchronized with seasonal factors such as changes in light and temperature.

As winter approaches, animals prepare for hibernation by eating large amounts of food which increases their body fat. As they prepare to hibernate, animals slowly stop shivering. Shivering, one of the body's responses to cold, helps maintain normal body temperature. When an animal stops shivering, its temperature decreases. Animals that enter hibernation also have a reduced heart rate and a slower blood flow to certain parts of the body, including the muscles. For example, during hibernation, a ground squirrel's heart rate decreases from 200 beats per minute to 4 or 5 per minute. The changes in shivering, blood flow, and heart rate are believed to be controlled by the hypothalamus in the brain. During hibernation, all animals maintain a body temperature high enough to permit tissues and organs to function.

As an animal wakes from hibernation, its temperature increases. At the same time, the animal's heart rate accelerates and its circulation increases. The animal can then leave its place of hibernation to find food and begin the next annual cycle.

Evaluation *On the lines provided, answer the following:*

1. How does an animal know when to hibernate?

_____

_____

2. Review the information you have been given about hibernation. In the space below, create a chart that shows the changes that occur in an animal's body as it prepares for hibernation, during hibernation, and when it wakes from hibernation.

Chapter 34 Animal Behavior   **Graphic Organizer**

Concept Map

Using information from the chapter, complete the concept map below. If there is not enough room in the concept map to write your answers, write them on a separate sheet of paper.

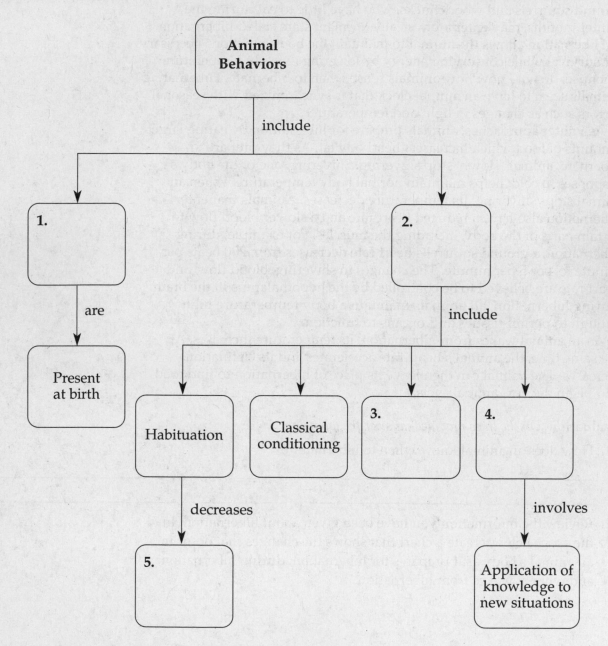

Multiple Choice

Write the letter that best answers the question or completes the statement on the line provided.

_____ 1. For a behavior to evolve under the influence of natural selection, that behavior must
   a. improve survival and reproduction.
   b. influence physical characteristics.
   c. be acquired through learning.
   d. be related to predator avoidance.

_____ 2. Animals that have very simple nervous systems cannot
   a. detect external stimuli.
   b. process information from their senses.
   c. respond to stimuli.
   d. exhibit complex behaviors.

_____ 3. Complex inborn behaviors include each of the following EXCEPT
   a. web-building in spiders.
   b. nest-building in birds.
   c. potato-washing in macaques.
   d. suckling of newborn mammals.

_____ 4. Insight learning is a form of behavior that
   a. is characterized by decreased responsiveness to unimportant stimuli.
   b. involves random responses that lead to either reward or punishment.
   c. involves applying something already learned to a new situation.
   d. is performed correctly without any previous experience.

_____ 5. In Pavlov's experiments on classical conditioning, dogs
   a. learned to associate food with salivation.
   b. learned to ring a bell whenever they were hungry.
   c. associated a new stimulus with a reward.
   d. were conditioned to produce an innate behavior in response to food.

_____ 6. When you use knowledge and experience to figure out why a lamp in your house will not light, you are using
   a. classical conditioning.
   b. insight learning.
   c. innate behavior.
   d. trial-and-error learning.

_____ 7. The type of learning that begins with a random behavior that is rewarded is called
   a. classical conditioning.   c. habituation.
   b. operant conditioning.   d. trial-and-error learning.

_____ 8. Imprinting is a form of behavior that
   a. is restricted to birds.
   b. is often used in the training of adult animals.
   c. occurs during a specific time in young animals.
   d. always involves the sense of sight.

_____ 9. After a young duck imprints on a nonliving model of an adult duck, the young duck will
   a. then imprint on its mother.
   b. then imprint on any real adult duck.
   c. follow only that model.
   d. follow any other kind of model.

_____10. An animal is most likely to enter into dormancy when
   a. it is advantageous to be active.
   b. resources are most difficult to find.
   c. food is very plentiful.
   d. the weather is very mild.

_____11. Animals are LEAST likely to migrate out of an area where
   a. there is little or no seasonal change in weather.
   b. food becomes scarce during part of the year.
   c. competition for resources increases during part of the year.
   d. winters are very cold and snowy.

_____12. It is advantageous for grazing mammals to gather in groups because groups
   a. can make the available food resources last longer.
   b. can migrate more easily than individuals can.
   c. are more difficult for predators to locate than individuals are.
   d. offer greater protection from predation.

_____13. In some species of balloon flies, males spin balloons of silk and carry them while flying. If a female approaches one of the males and accepts his balloon, the two will fly off to mate. This type of behavior is an example of
   a. aggression.   c. courtship.
   b. territorial defense.   d. language.

_____14. Competition for limited resources can involve each of the following EXCEPT
   a. rituals.   c. displays.
   b. circadian rhythms.   d. aggression.

____15. Nocturnal animals that have a poorly developed sense of
smell are most likely to communicate by
a. sound signals.   c. pheromones.
b. visual displays.   d. chemical signals.

Completion

Complete each statement on the line provided.

16. A snail will withdraw into its shell if it is prodded with a sharp object. In this behavior, prodding is the _____ and the snail's withdrawal is the response.

17. If a dog learns to ignore vehicles that drive past its house without stopping, the dog's behavior has probably been altered through the type of learning known as _____ .

18. For an animal to become habituated to a stimulus, the stimulus must NOT be either _____ or rewarding.

19. When an animal associates a stimulus with a reward or punishment, it learns by the process known as _____ .

20. If an animal produces a sound and another animal obtains information by hearing the sound, the two animals are engaging in a form of _____ .

Short Answer

In complete sentences, write the answers to the questions on the lines provided.

21. Why are innate behaviors important? Explain.

_____

_____

_____

_____

22. How is habituation useful to an animal?

_____

_____

_____

_____

23. Explain how imprinting in young geese involves both innate and learned behavior.

_____

_____

_____

_____

24. Explain why dormancy and migration are beneficial.

_____

_____

_____

_____

25. Why is it an evolutionary advantage for an animal in a society to help other members of the society?

_____

_____

_____

_____

Using Science Skills

Use the diagram below to answer the questions on the following page on the lines provided.

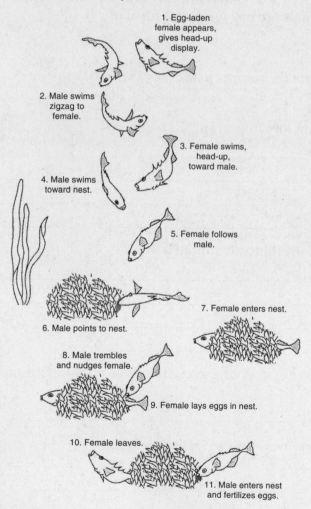

Courtship Behavior of Sticklebacks

1. Egg-laden female appears, gives head-up display.

2. Male swims zigzag to female.

3. Female swims, head-up, toward male.

4. Male swims toward nest.

5. Female follows male.

6. Male points to nest.

7. Female enters nest.

8. Male trembles and nudges female.

9. Female lays eggs in nest.

10. Female leaves.

11. Male enters nest and fertilizes eggs.

Figure 1

26. **Applying Concepts** Even if young sticklebacks never observe the courtship of other sticklebacks, they can perform the courtship behavior shown in Figure 1. Is the courtship behavior innate or learned?

_____

27. **Interpreting Graphics** According to Figure 1, which member of the pair of stickleback fish begins the courtship?

_____

28. **Inferring** In Figure 1, determine from the action of the sticklebacks whether the nest is built by the male or the female. Explain.

_____

_____

29. **Interpreting Graphics** In Figure 1, what stimuli does the male stickleback give to the female during courtship?

_____

_____

_____

30. **Interpreting Graphics** In Figure 1, what stimuli does the female stickleback give to the male during courtship?

_____

_____

_____

Essay

Write the answer to each question in the space provided.

31. Explain how behaviors can evolve under the influence of natural selection.

32. Contrast classical and operant conditioning.

33. Describe a Skinner box and explain what it is used for.

34. Explain the adaptive advantages of a territory to the animal that establishes it.

35. Explain how it is possible for animals to communicate without having language and what kinds of information animals communicate with nonverbal signals.

Chapter 34 Animal Behavior

Multiple Choice

Write the letter that best answers the question or completes the statement on the line provided.

_____ 1. A stimulus is a(an)
   a. reaction to an external event.
   b. reaction to an internal event.
   c. internal or external signal.

_____ 2. When disturbed, certain moths lift their front wings to expose eyelike markings on their hind wings. This behavior would be most effective against predators that hunt by
   a. sound.
   b. smell.
   c. sight.

_____ 3. Which of the following terms is NOT closely related to the others?
   a. innate behavior
   b. learned behavior
   c. inborn behavior

_____ 4. Trial-and-error learning is also known as
   a. operant conditioning.
   b. insight learning.
   c. classical conditioning.

_____ 5. The process in which an animal stops responding to a repetitive stimulus is called
   a. habituation.
   b. classical conditioning.
   c. operant conditioning.

_____ 6. Any change in which a behavior is altered as a result of experience is called
   a. habituation.
   b. operant conditioning.
   c. learning.

_____ 7. For young geese to imprint on an object, that object must
   a. move.
   b. be some kind of animal.
   c. look like an adult goose.

_____ **8.** The ability of salmon to recognize their home stream at spawning time is an example of
   a. insight learning.
   b. habituation.
   c. imprinting.

_____ **9.** A circadian rhythm is a cycle that
   a. is related to the phase of the moon.
   b. is related to the temperature of the air.
   c. has a daily pattern.

_____ **10.** Migration is a behavior that is usually influenced by
   a. changing seasons.
   b. the phase of the moon.
   c. the rise and fall of tides.

_____ **11.** Which of the following is NOT a type of social behavior?
   a. courtship
   b. habituation
   c. hunting in a pack

_____ **12.** The members of a society
   a. belong to at least two species.
   b. exhibit a type of social behavior.
   c. act independently for each individual's benefit.

_____ **13.** The resources in a territory can include all of the following EXCEPT
   a. food.
   b. nesting sites.
   c. predators.

_____ **14.** Dolphins communicate with one another mainly through
   a. sound.
   b. visual displays.
   c. chemical signals.

_____ **15.** A pheromone is a type of
   a. visual signal.
   b. sound signal.
   c. chemical messenger.

Completion

Complete each statement on the line provided.

16. A single, specific reaction to a stimulus is called a(an) _____ .

17. The Russian scientist named _____ studied conditioning in dogs.

18. The most complicated form of learning is _____ learning.

19. When competing for a territory, animals may show _____ to gain control over each other.

20. Only humans are known to use _____ , a complex system of communication that uses sounds, symbols, and gestures according to a set of rules.

Short Answer

In complete sentences, write the answers to the questions on the lines provided.

21. What body systems are involved when an animal responds to a stimulus?

_____

_____

_____

_____

_____

22. Define *innate behavior*.

_____

_____

_____

_____

_____

_____

23. List the four major types of learning.

_____

_____

_____

24. What are the functions of courtship?

_____

_____

_____

_____

_____

_____

25. List the types of signals animals may use to communicate with one another.

_____

_____

_____

_____

Using Science Skills

Use the diagram below to answer the following questions on the lines provided.

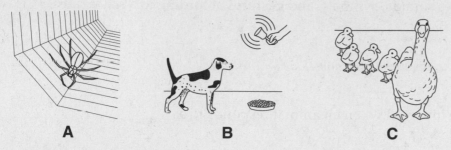

A   **B**   **C**

Figure 1

26. **Interpreting Graphics** In Figure 1, what type of behavior does drawing A show?

_____

_____

_____

27. **Interpreting Graphics** In Figure 1, what type of learning does drawing B show?

_____

_____

_____

28. **Interpreting Graphics** In Figure 1, identify the two stimuli that are involved in drawing B. Also, identify the response that will be produced in drawing B.

_____

_____

_____

_____

29. **Applying Concepts** Which of the four major types of learning is(are) NOT shown in Figure 1?

_____

_____

_____

_____

30. **Interpreting Graphics** In Figure 1, what behavioral process does drawing C show?

_____

_____

_____

Multiple Choice

Write the letter that best answers the question or completes the statement on the line provided.

_____ **1.** Which of the following statements about chordates is true?

    a. All chordates are vertebrates.

    b. All chordates have backbones.

    c. All chordates have a notochord.

    d. All chordates have paired appendages.

_____ **2.** The eggs of ovoviviparous fish are

    a. released from the female immediately after being fertilized.

    b. retained and nourished by the female.

    c. released from the female before they are fertilized.

    d. held inside the female's body as they develop.

_____ **3.** Which of the following structures are found in the adult frog but not in the tadpole?

    a. gills   c. single-loop circulatory system

    b. three-chambered heart   d. all of the above

_____ **4.** Reptiles are successful on land because of

    a. amniotic eggs.

    b. a single-loop circulatory system.

    c. endothermy.

    d. external fertilization.

_____ **5.** Which structure in the amniotic egg provides nutrients for the embryo as it grows?

    a. amnion   c. allantois

    b. chorion   d. yolk

_____ **6.** A characteristic of birds but not reptiles is

    a. urine excreted as uric acid.

    b. air sacs.

    c. an amniotic egg.

    d. a cloaca.

_____ **7.** Which of the following is NOT a characteristic of mammals?

    a. ability to nourish their young with milk

    b. scaly skin

    c. hair

    d. endothermy

_____ **8.** The mammals in the figure above have similar characteristics because

    a. they are closely related.

    b. they have adapted to different environments on the same continent.

    c. of divergent evolution.

    d. of convergent evolution.

_____ **9.** The hominoid group of primates includes

    a. prosimians and anthropoids.

    b. New World monkeys and Old World monkeys.

    c. apes and hominids.

    d. anthropoids only.

_____**10.** Endothermy is characterized by

    a. requiring large amounts of food.

    b. a low metabolic rate.

    c. behaviors that help regulate body temperature.

    d. a lack of insulating feathers, fat, or hair.

_____**11.** A single-loop circulatory system is present in all animals with

    a. jaws.   c. a backbone.

    b. a four-chambered heart.   d. gills.

_____**12.** Which of the following trends in reproduction is evident as you move through the vertebrate groups?

    a. external fertilization to internal fertilization

    b. endothermy to ectothermy

    c. progressively fewer openings in the digestive tract

    d. closed circulatory system to open circulatory system

_____**13.** When a bird learns to press a button to get food, it has learned by

    a. habituation.

    b. classical conditioning.

    c. operant conditioning.

    d. insight learning.

_____**14.** Sea turtles that travel each spring from their feeding grounds to their nesting grounds are

    a. courting.   c. socializing.

    b. migrating.   d. communicating.

_____ **15.** When a lion snaps, claws, and snarls at the other lions before settling down to eat, it is
   a. showing aggression.
   b. communicating.
   c. competing.
   d. all of the above

Completion

Complete each statement on the line provided.

16. A vertebrate with moist skin that contains mucous glands, and lacks scales and claws is a(an) _____.

17. Unlike other reptiles, crocodiles and alligators have a(an) _____ heart like birds and mammals.

18. The first true mammals appeared during the late _____, about 220 million years ago.

19. All chordates, both invertebrate and vertebrate, share a common _____ ancestor.

20. When a dog barks at a ringing doorbell, the barking is the _____ and the ringing doorbell is the _____.

Short Answer

In complete sentences, write the answers to the questions on the lines provided.

21. Why are tunicates and lancelets classified as chordates even though they are invertebrates?

_____

_____

_____

22. Why are amphibians dependent on water?

_____

_____

_____

_____

23. What adaptations do birds have for flight?

_____

_____

_____

24. What characteristics do all primates share?

_____

_____

_____

25. How is a behavior produced in an animal?

_____

_____

_____

Using Science Skills

Use the diagram below to answer the following questions on the lines provided.

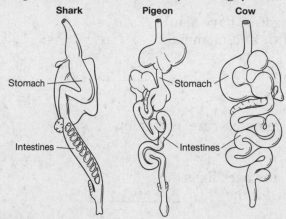

26. Interpreting Graphics Which vertebrate digestive system shown above has the largest stomach?

_____

_____

27. Interpreting Graphics Which of the vertebrates shown above are carnivores? Which are herbivores? Explain.

_____

_____

_____

28. Applying Concepts Why are the digestive systems of birds and mammals more complex than the digestive system of fishes?

_____

_____

_____

29. Applying Concepts What structures are found only in the pigeon's digestive system? What digestive functions do these structures have?

_____

_____

_____

30. Inferring Describe the structure of the cow's teeth. Relate teeth structure to their function.

_____

_____

Essay

Write the answer to each question in the space provided.

31. Compare hominid evolution with the evolution of other chordate groups.

32. Relate the complexity of human communication and the structure of the human nervous system and sense organs.

33. Compare the structures of the respiratory systems in all vertebrate groups.

34. Explain how the control of body temperature is important for maintaining homeostasis.

35. How does an animal's behavior make it better adapted to its environment?

Unit 9 Chordates | Unit Test B

Multiple Choice

Write the letter that best answers the question or completes the statement on the line provided.

_____ 1.. Which of the following is NOT a characteristic of all chordates?

    a. dorsal, hollow nerve cord

    b. tail that extends past the anus

    c. vertebrae

_____ 2. All of the following are examples of cartilaginous fishes EXCEPT

    a. skates.

    b. hagfishes.

    c. sharks.

_____ 3. The presence of lungs enables adult amphibians to

    a. breathe under water.

    b. take in carbon dioxide.

    c. live on land.

_____ 4. One way in which reptiles are adapted to a fully terrestrial life is

    a. external fertilization.

    b. an amniotic egg.

    c. endothermy.

_____ 5. Compared with that of a reptile, a bird's body temperature is

    a. higher and more constant.

    b. higher and more variable.

    c. lower and more constant.

_____ 6. The single most important characteristic that separates birds from other chordates is

    a. the amniotic egg.

    b. wings.

    c. feathers.

_____ 7. Characteristics of mammals include all of the following EXCEPT

    a. ectothermy.

    b. hair.

    c. lungs.

_____ **8.** Mammals that lay eggs are called
    a. monotremes.
    b. marsupials.
    c. placentals.

_____ **9.** The two main groups of primates are
    a. Old World monkeys and New World monkeys.
    b. apes and humans.
    c. prosimians and anthropoids.

_____**10.** Which of the following animals are ectotherms?
    a. shark and ostrich
    b. salamander and rattlesnake
    c. duckbill platypus and crocodile

_____**11.** The vertebrate group with the most efficient respiratory system is
    a. mammals.
    b. reptiles.
    c. birds.

_____**12.** A double-loop circulatory system is present in all animals with
    a. lungs.
    b. vertebrae.
    c. a two-chambered heart.

_____**13.** An innate behavior
    a. appears in fully functional form the first time it is performed.
    b. requires habituation.
    c. occurs with trial and error.

_____**14.** When an animal associates a stimulus with a reward or a
    punishment, it has learned by
    a. habituation.
    b. classical conditioning.
    c. operant conditioning.

_____**15.** An animal that communicates visually will have
    a. good hearing.
    b. a good sense of smell.
    c. good eyesight.

Completion

Complete each statement on the line provided.

16. The evolution of _____ and _____ were
    important developments during the rise of fishes.

Name______________________________ Class__________________ Date ______________

17. Turtles and tortoises are characterized by a ________________ built into the skeleton, which is used for protection.

18. The evolution of a(an) ________________ enabled hominids to grasp objects and use tools.

19. A(An) ________________ is an animal whose body temperature is controlled from within.

20. When you get up to answer the telephone, the ________________ is the ringing telephone and the ________________ is getting up to answer it.

Short Answer

In complete sentences, write the answers to the questions on the lines provided.

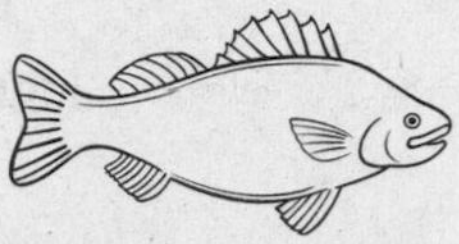

Figure 1

21. Is the chordate in Figure 1 adapted to an aquatic or a terrestrial lifestyle? How do you know?

____

____

____

22. What similarities between reptiles and birds lead scientists to think that birds evolved from extinct reptiles?

____

____

____

23. How do mammalian kidneys help maintain homeostasis?

____

____

____

24. Briefly describe two evolutionary trends scientists use to describe the evolution of chordates.

____

____

____

25. How do social behaviors increase an animal's evolutionary fitness?

____

____

____

Using Science Skills

Use the diagram below to answer the following questions on the lines provided.

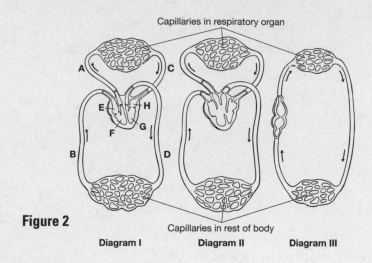

Figure 2

26. **Interpreting Graphics** Which of the diagrams in Figure 2 illustrate(s) a single-loop circulatory system?

_____

27. **Applying Concepts** Which of the circulatory systems in Figure 2 support(s) gills and which support(s) lungs?

_____
_____

28. **Interpreting Graphics** What is the difference between the heart in Diagram I and the heart in Diagram II?

_____
_____
_____
_____
_____

29. **Interpreting Graphics** What vertebrate group is characterized by the circulatory system shown in Diagram II?

_____
_____

30. **Inferring** Which of the circulatory systems in Figure 2 is most efficient at providing body tissues with oxygen? Explain.

_____
_____
_____

Chapter 30 Nonvertebrate Chordates, Fishes, and Amphibians

Answers for the Adapted Reading and Study Workbook (worksheets pp. 7–15) can be found in the Adapted Reading and Study Workbook, Annotated Teacher's Edition.

Answers for the Reading and Study Workbook (worksheets pp. 18–27) can be found in the Reading and Study Workbook, Annotated Teacher's Edition.

Section Review 30-1

1. nerve cord **2.** pharyngeal pouches **3.** notochord **4.** notochord **5.** tail **6.** pharyngeal pouches **7.** Unlike most chordates, lancelets and tunicates do not have a backbone and are therefore classified as nonvertebrate chordates. **8.** Unlike adult tunicates, adult lancelets have a definite head and mouth. **9.** Most adult chordates do not have a notochord. This characteristic is seen only in the embryonic stage of development for most chordates. **10.** If the organism is a chordate, it should have the following characteristics at some point in its life: a dorsal, hollow nerve cord; a notochord; pharyngeal pouches; and a tail that extends beyond the anus.

Section Review 30-2

1. paired fins, gills, scales **2.** paired fins **3.** herbivores, carnivores **4.** lungs **5.** cartilaginous **6.** jawless **7.** bony **8.** In both methods, the embryos develop inside the mother's body. In ovoviviparous fishes the embryos obtain food from the yolk. In viviparous fishes, the mother's body nourishes the young until they are ready to be born. **9.** Both types of fishes spend part of their lives in fresh water and part of their lives in salt water. Anadromous fishes migrate to fresh water to breed, and catadromous fishes migrate to salt water to breed. **10.** Jawed fishes can eat a wider variety of food than jawless fishes. They can also defend themselves by biting.

Section Review 30-3

1. in water **2.** lungs **3.** moist **4.** lack **5.** Stronger bones and limb girdles enabled more efficient movement; lungs and breathing tubes enabled amphibians to breathe air; the sternum provided protection and support for internal organs. **6.** caecilians **7.** frogs and toads **8.** salamanders **9.** The left atrium brings oxygen-rich blood from the skin and lungs into the heart. The right atrium brings oxygen-poor blood from the rest of the body into the heart. While there is some mixing, most oxygen-poor blood goes to the lungs, and most oxygen-rich blood goes to the rest of the body. **10.** Amphibians depend on water to keep their eggs moist. The larvae of amphibians, lacking lungs to breathe air, also need to develop in water. As the environmental water and moisture decreased, many species of amphibians died out.

Chapter Vocabulary Review

1. cerebrum **2.** cerebellum **3.** medulla oblongata **4.** chordate **5.** notochord **6.** pharyngeal pouches **7.** cartilage **8.** vertebra **9.** atrium **10.** ventricle **11.** cerebellum **12.** cerebrum **13.** lateral line system **14.** swim bladder **15.** oviparous **16.** ovoviviparous **17.** viviparous **18.** cloaca **19.** nictitating membrane **20.** tympanic membranes

Enrichment

1. Sample answer: Few sharks pose a serious threat to humans. Only a few species, such as the great white or the hammerhead, have been known to attack humans. On the other hand, sharks are an important part of the ocean ecosystem. They rid the sea of dead and dying fishes. They control populations of bottom-dwelling organisms. **2.** Possible answers include: Their acute sense of smell helps sharks to locate prey. Other sharks can detect the electrical stimuli produced by most fishes.

Graphic Organizer

1–2. Notochord, Pharyngeal pouches **3.** Vertebrates **4–5.** Tunicates, Lancelets **6.** Fishes **7.** Amphibians **8.** Birds

Chapter 30—Test A

Multiple Choice 1. C **2.** D **3.** D **4.** B **5.** C **6.** A **7.** B **8.** D **9.** B **10.** A **11.** D **12.** C **13.** D **14.** C **15.** D **Completion 16.** pharyngeal pouches **17.** gills **18.** amphibian **19.** drying out **20.** right atrium **Short Answer 21.** The front end grows into a brain. **22.** bodies that were armored with bony plates **23.** The pyloric ceca are fingerlike pouches located near the stomach. They secrete digestive enzymes and absorb nutrients from digested food. **24.** Anadromous fishes spend most of their lives in the ocean but migrate to fresh water to breed, whereas catadromous fishes live their lives in fresh water but migrate to the ocean to breed. **25.** A—cartilage, B—bone, C—fibers and cartilage **Using Science Skills 26.** A is the sinus venosus, B is the atrium, C is the ventricle, and D is the bulbus arteriosus. **27.** It is poor in oxygen. **28.** C, the ventricle, is the actual pumping portion. **29.** the aorta **30.** the gills **Essay 31.** An adult lancelet is a fishlike animal with a hollow nerve cord, a notochord, and segmented muscles that run the length of the body. It has a definite head region and a tail. An adult tunicate has a body that is covered by a tough, nonliving tunic. The tunic is flattened at the base, where the animal is typically attached to a solid surface, and it has two large openings called siphons. An adult tunicate does not have a hollow nerve cord, a notochord, segmented muscles, a head region, or a tail. **32.** Because jaws could hold teeth and muscles, jaws made it possible for these fishes to chew on plants and other animals. Thus, fishes with jaws could eat a much wider variety of food than could jawless fishes. Jaws also allowed fishes to defend themselves by biting. **33.** The main parts are the olfactory bulbs, cerebrum, optic lobes, cerebellum, and medulla oblongata. The olfactory bulbs and cerebrum are both involved with the sense of smell, or olfaction. The optic lobes process information from the eyes. The cerebellum coordinates body movements. The medulla oblongata controls the functioning of many internal organs. **34.** The number of living species of amphibians in the world is decreasing. Possible explanations for the decline include environmental threats, such as decreasing habitat, depletion of the ozone layer, acid rain, water pollution, fungal infections, introduced aquatic predators, and an increasing human population. **35.** Adult amphibians have a double-loop circulatory system and a heart with three chambers. One loop carries oxygen-poor blood from the ventricle to the lungs and takes oxygen-rich blood from the lungs to the left atrium. The left atrium empties this blood into the ventricle. The other loop transports oxygen-rich blood from the ventricle to the rest of the body and oxygen-poor blood from the body to the right atrium. The right atrium also empties its blood into the ventricle.

Chapter 30—Test B

Multiple Choice **1.** B **2.** A **3.** A **4.** A **5.** B **6.** A **7.** B **8.** A **9.** C **10.** A **11.** C **12.** B **13.** A **14.** B **15.** C **Completion** **16.** vertebrae **17.** cartilage **18.** smell **19.** Amphibians **20.** three **Short Answer** **21.** a dorsal, hollow nerve cord; a notochord; pharyngeal pouches; and a tail that extends beyond the anus **22.** Lancelets move in a fishlike motion by contracting muscles on either side of the body. **23.** A, a shark, is a cartilaginous fish (class Chondrichthyes), B is a bony fish (class Osteichthyes), and C is a jawless fish (a lamprey). **24.** Accept any two: strong bones in the limbs and limb girdles; lungs and breathing tubes to breathe air; ribs form a bony cage that support and protect internal organs against the pull of gravity. **25.** salamanders, frogs and toads, and caecilians **Using Science Skills** **26.** the notochord **27.** the dorsal hollow nerve cord **28.** the tail **29.** pharyngeal pouches

30. They develop slits that connect to the outside of the body. The slits may then develop into gills.

Chapter 31 Reptiles and Birds

Answers for the Adapted Reading and Study Workbook (worksheets pp. 50–56) can be found in the Adapted Reading and Study Workbook, Annotated Teacher's Edition.

Answers for the Reading and Study Workbook (worksheets pp. 59–66) can be found in the Reading and Study Workbook, Annotated Teacher's Edition.

Section Review 31-1

1. Yes **2.** Yes **3.** Yes **4.** No **5.** No **6.** Yes **7.** No **8.** Turtles and tortoises **9.** Crocodilians **10.** Lizards and snakes **11.** Tuataras **12.** Reptiles that live on land convert ammonia to uric acid, which is less toxic. **13.** Advantage: The scaly skin of reptiles is protective and prevents the loss of body water in dry environments. Disadvantage: The skin does not grow as the reptile grows, so the reptile must periodically shed the old layer of skin as it grows. **14.** The amnion produces a protected, watery environment that surrounds and cushions the embryo. The chorion regulates the transport of oxygen and carbon dioxide. The yolk sac contains the nutrient-rich food supply for the embryo. The allantois stores the waste produced by the embryo. **15.** Both reptiles and amphibians have strong limbs and limb girdles for moving on land. The legs of some reptiles are also rotated further under the body than those of amphibians, enabling reptiles to carry more body weight.

Section Review 31-2

1. constant **2.** feathers **3.** chest **4.** This adaptation is a feather. Feathers provide birds with the lifting force and balance needed for flight. **5.** The wing is a modified front limb. The structure of the wing is aerodynamic and enables flight. **6.** A bird's circulatory system consists of a four-chambered heart and a double loop circulatory system. This system completely separates oxygen-poor and oxygen-rich blood so that the body receives enough oxygen for the energy requirements of flight. **7.** The lungs and air sacs of a bird are designed so that there is a one-way flow of air through the lungs. **8.** Possible answers include: Strong, hooked bills allow carnivorous birds to shred their prey; large, long bills help birds pick fruit; flat bills help with grasping fish. **9.** Yes. Since birds do not have teeth and they cannot chew, this bird must have some other method to help with the mechanical breakdown of insects and seeds. A gizzard is a muscular organ that crushes food, making it easier to digest. **10.** Flat feathers are streamlined and present little resistance to airflow.

Chapter Vocabulary Review

1. crop **2.** plastron **3.** carapace **4.** air sac
5. endotherm **6.** gizzard **7.** amniotic **8.** feather
9. ectotherm **10.** b **11.** c **12.** d **13.** c **14.** b **15.** a
16. a **17.** b **18.** a **19.** d **20.** d

Enrichment

1. No. Some birds, such as the house sparrow, do not migrate at all. **2.** Advantages of migration are availability of food and other resources that exist only part of the year; disadvantages of migration include the tremendous energy cost associated with long flights, and the chance of death. **3.** Birds' hormonal cycles include an "annual clock." When the climatic conditions and the length of daylight change appropriately, birds begin their migration.

Graphic Organizer

1. Turtles **2.** Tortoises **3.** Crocodiles **4.** Tuataras
5. Fresh water **6.** Lizards **7.** Snakes

Chapter 31—Test A

Multiple Choice **1.** D **2.** A **3.** D **4.** A **5.** C **6.** A
7. D **8.** B **9.** C **10.** B **11.** B **12.** C **13.** A **14.** C
15. C **Completion** **16.** extinction **17.** amniotic
18. energy **19.** four **20.** magnetic **Short Answer**
21. A reptile's skin does not grow when the rest of the reptile grows. Reptiles overcome this disadvantage by shedding their skin periodically as they increase in size. **22.** The lungs of reptiles have more gas-exchange area than those of amphibians.
23. Student answers may include: Many reptiles in this order (turtles and tortoises) can pull their head, legs, and tail into their shells to protect themselves. They also have jaws that are often powerful enough to deliver a damaging bite. **24.** Structure A (the collarbone) consists of bones that are fused together. It is therefore more rigid than the corresponding structure in other vertebrates. **25.** In flying birds, Structure B (the sternum or breastbone) is enlarged and has a long keel that provides an attachment site for the large chest muscles that are necessary for flight.
Using Science Skills **26.** The bird labeled A probably eats insects because it has a short, fine bill that can pick insects off surfaces or catch them as they fly. **27.** The long, thin bill is adapted to probing soft mud for worms and other invertebrates. **28.** The bird labeled C probably eats meat because its strong, hooked bill can tear and shred prey. **29.** This bird would not be successful at eating insects because its large bill would not be fine enough to pick insects off leaves and branches. **30.** The bird labeled E probably eats seeds because its short, thick bill can be used for

breaking open seeds. **Essay** **31.** Dinosaurs ranged in size from small to enormous. Some walked on two legs, and others walked on four. Some ate leafy plants, and others hunted in large herds. Some dinosaurs lived in small family groups and cared for their young in nests. Certain dinosaurs may even have had feathers. **32.** Both lizards and alligators have a double-loop circulatory system and a heart with two atria. One of the loops sends blood to the lungs and returns it to the left atrium. The other loop sends blood to the rest of the body and returns that blood to the right atrium. In a lizard, there is a single ventricle with a partial internal wall that helps separate oxygen-rich and oxygen-poor blood. In an alligator, there are two ventricles, so oxygen-rich and oxygen-poor blood remain completely separated.
33. *Archaeopteryx* looked like a small, running dinosaur, but it had well-developed feathers covering most of its body. The presence of feathers supports the classification of *Archaeopteryx* as a bird. However, *Archaeopteryx* also had teeth in its beak, a bony tail, and toes and claws on its wings, all of which are features that modern birds lack. Taken together, the current evidence indicates that *Archaeopteryx* was a transitional species with characteristics of both dinosaurs and birds. **34.** When a bird inhales, most air first enters large air sacs in the body cavity and bones. The inhaled air then flows to the lungs and travels through the lungs in a series of small tubes. This system ensures that air flows into the air sacs and out through the lungs in a single direction, which constantly exposes the lungs to oxygen-rich air. This constant exposure helps birds maintain a high metabolic rate and provides the oxygen necessary for high-altitude flight. **35.** Hummingbirds and other nectar-eating birds transfer pollen from flower to flower as they feed, thereby pollinating flowers. Fruit-eating birds swallow seeds but may not digest them, so their droppings disperse seeds over great distances. Insect-eating birds, such as swallows and chimney swifts, catch great numbers of mosquitoes and other insects, thereby helping control insect populations. Many other examples would be acceptable.

Chapter 31—Test B

Multiple Choice **1.** B **2.** B **3.** C **4.** C **5.** C **6.** C
7. D **8.** B **9.** A **10.** A **11.** B **12.** C **13.** A **14.** C
15. B **Completion** **16.** cloaca **17.** plastron
18. collarbone (or wishbone) **19.** sternum (or breast bone) **20.** seeds **Short Answer** **21.** Uric acid is much less toxic than ammonia, so it does not have to be diluted with as much water. Therefore, water is conserved in the bodies of land reptiles. **22.** Sample answer: Many reptiles are in danger because their

habitats have been and are being destroyed. Humans also hunt reptiles for food, to sell as pets, and for their skins. **23.** Birds are endotherms, which means that they generate their own body heat through their metabolism by eating food. **24.** One explanation is that birds evolved directly from dinosaurs. A second explanation is that both dinosaurs and birds evolved from a common ancestor. **25.** Possible answers include hooked bills, large wingspans, or sharp talons. **Using Science Skills 26.** the amnion; It is a fluid-filled sac that surrounds and cushions the developing embryo. **27.** the allantois; It stores the waste produced by the embryo and also serves as a respiratory organ. **28.** the chorion; It regulates the transport of oxygen and carbon dioxide between the embryo and the surface of the egg. **29.** the yolk sac; It contains yolk, the food supply for the embryo. **30.** the shell; It is soft and leathery in most reptile eggs.

Chapter 32 Mammals

Answers for the Adapted Reading and Study Workbook (worksheets pp. 89–96) can be found in the Adapted Reading and Study Workbook, Annotated Teacher's Edition.

Answers for the Reading and Study Workbook (worksheets pp. 99–108) can be found in the Reading and Study Workbook, Annotated Teacher's Edition.

Section Review 32-1

1. Yes **2.** No **3.** Yes **4.** No **5.** Yes **6.** The first true mammals appeared during the late Triassic Period, about 220 million years ago. **7.** As mammals evolved, the form and function of their jaws and teeth became adapted to eat foods other than insects. **8.** Kidneys help maintain homeostasis in mammals by filtering urea from the blood and by maintaining water balance in the body. **9.** A mammal requires about ten times as much food as a reptile of the same size. To use all the energy in that food, it is reasonable to assume that the mammal would need more oxygen than the reptile. **10.** Carnivores have much sharper canines than herbivores, molars and premolars that interlock like scissors during chewing. Herbivores have broad, flat molars and premolars that are adapted for grinding tough plant material.

Section Review 32-2

1. monotremes **2.** placentals **3.** marsupials **4.** marsupials **5.** placentals **6.** monotremes **7.** monotremes **8.** Young monotremes lick milk from pores on the mother's abdomen. **9.** A marsupium is an external pouch on the mother's body, into which the marsupial embryo crawls and completes its development. **10.** The placenta allows the exchange of nutrients, oxygen, carbon dioxide, and wastes between the embryo and the mother. **11.** The drifting apart of Earth's single landmass into separate continents set the stage for the convergent evolution of mammals. **12.** monotreme **13.** marsupial **14.** placental **15.** placental

Section Review 32-3

1. binocular vision **2.** cerebral cortex or cerebrum **3.** shoulder **4.** fingers, toes **5.** prosimians, anthropoids **6.** adaptive radiations **7.** New World monkeys have long, flexible arms and a long, prehensile tail. Old World monkeys lack prehensile tails. **8.** Bipedal locomotion freed both hands for using tools. An opposable thumb enabled the grasping of objects and the use of tools. **9.** Paleontologists frequently revise their ideas about hominid evolution because the discovery of new fossils makes them reevaluate their inferences. **10.** DNA analysis shows that modern nonhuman primates and modern humans have very similar DNA.

Chapter Vocabulary Review

1. e **2.** a **3.** f **4.** g **5.** c **6.** h **7.** b **8.** d **9.** j **10.** i **11.** monotremes **12.** marsupials **13.** placenta **14.** anthropoids **15.** opposable **16.** c **17.** d **18.** a **19.** c **20.** a

Enrichment

1. Possible answers include: To observe and learn about the natural behavior of animals, scientists often try to observe their subjects without influencing their behavior. When a scientist is not primarily concerned with natural behavior, it might be necessary to interact with the subject. **2.** Possible answers include: Both Goodall and Fossey studied the behavior of primates in their natural environments. Unlike Goodall, Fossey also became an environmental activist who used aggressive methods.

Graphic Organizer

1. Monotremes **2.** Placental mammals **3.** Marsupium (or pouch) **4.** Artiodactyls **5.** Primates **6.** Carnivores **7.** Insects

Chapter 32—Test A

Multiple Choice 1. B **2.** A **3.** A **4.** C **5.** B **6.** C **7.** C **8.** B **9.** B **10.** C **11.** A **12.** B **13.** B **14.** C **15.** A **Completion 16.** mammary glands **17.** insects **18.** placenta **19.** bipedal **20.** anthropoids **Short Answer 21.** Mammals have a lower jaw consisting of a teeth-bearing bone connected by a joint directly to the skull, and distinctive features of the limbs and the backbone. **22.** The rumen is a stomach chamber that stores and processes newly swallowed plant food. Bacteria in the rumen break down the hard-to-digest cellulose of plant tissues. Carnivores do not have rumens because digestive enzymes alone can quickly digest meat. **23.** Mammals maintain homeostasis by regulating their body heat and excreting or retaining water with the kidneys. **24.** After the embryo is born, it crawls across its mother's fur and attaches to a nipple. In most marsupials, the nipples are located in a pouch called the marsupium. The young marsupial continues to grow and develop while attached to the nipple, until it is large enough to survive on its own. **25.** Binocular vision provides depth perception, which is important for judging the locations of tree branches. **Using Science Skills** **26.** artiodactyls **27.** perissodactyls **28.** The bones are slender, reducing the wing's weight. The "fingers" are spread out to support flaps of skin that form a wing. **29.** The bones are much thicker than the bat's. **30.** The long, slender snout is adapted to probe into the ground, looking for ants. **Essay** **31.** Mammals have a high rate of metabolism, which helps them generate body heat. Mammals also have body hair and subcutaneous fat, which help them conserve heat. Many mammals have sweat glands that cool the body when the sweat evaporates from the skin. Mammals that lack sweat glands often pant when they need to rid themselves of excess heat. **32.** Specialized teeth and digestive systems process food more quickly and more thoroughly so that mammals can get the most nutrients from their food. This is important because mammals require a lot of energy to maintain their high metabolic rate. **33.** Monotremes have a cloaca, a structure into which the reproductive and urinary systems open, as do reptiles. Like most reptiles, monotremes also lay eggs. Like other mammals, monotremes nourish their young with milk produced by mammary glands. **34.** Both groups of monkeys are anthropoids. New World monkeys are found in Central and South America. They live almost entirely in trees and have long, flexible arms and long, prehensile tails. Old World Monkeys are found in Africa and Asia. They also spend time in trees but lack prehensile tails. **35.** Paleontologists once thought that hominid evolution ocurred in a simple, straight-line transformation of one species into another. Now, however, they think that hominid evolution occurred as a series of complex adaptive radiations that produced a large number of different species. Paleontologists changed their way of thinking as the result of many recent fossil finds.

Chapter 32—Test B

Multiple Choice **1.** A **2.** B **3.** A **4.** C **5.** A **6.** B **7.** C **8.** A **9.** C **10.** B **11.** C **12.** A **13.** C **14.** A **15.** B **Completion** **16.** hair **17.** duckbill platypus

18. cerebrum (or cerebral cortex) **19.** New World **20.** opposable **Short Answer** **21.** canines, incisors, molars, and premolars **22.** The diaphragm pulls the bottom of the chest cavity downward, increasing the volume of the cavity and drawing air into the lungs. **23.** the way mammals reproduce and develop **24.** A marsupium is a pouch on the outside of a female marsupial's body in which embryos complete their development. **25.** A prosimian is a type of primate that is generally small and nocturnal and has large eyes that are adapted to seeing in the dark. **Using Science Skills** **26.** II is the skull of a carnivore, and I is the skull of an herbivore. **27.** molars and premolars; They are used to crush and grind tough plants. **28.** incisors; They are used for cutting, gnawing, grooming and to grasp and tear vegetation. **29.** canines; They are used for piercing, gripping, slicing, and tearing flesh from prey. **30.** In the herbivore (mammal I), the jaws generally move from side to side. In the carnivore (mammal II), the jaws usually move up and down.

Chapter 33 Comparing Chordates

Answers for the Adapted Reading and Study Workbook (worksheets pp. 132–138) can be found in the Adapted Reading and Study Workbook, Annotated Teacher's Edition.

Answers for the Reading and Study Workbook (worksheets pp. 141–148) can be found in the Reading and Study Workbook, Annotated Teacher's Edition.

Section Review 33-1

1. a notochord, a dorsal hollow nerve cord, a tail that extends beyond the anus, and pharyngeal pouches **2.** *Pikaia* is considered the first chordate. It was classified as a chordate because it had a notochord. **3.** Vertebrates share a common ancestor with tunicates and lancelets. **4.** Adaptive radiations have been launched by the appearance of new adaptations, such as jaws and paired appendages. **5.** The adaptations appeared in the following order: vertebrae, jaws, lungs, four limbs, endothermy. **6.** adaptive radiation **7.** convergent evolution **8.** vertebrates **9.** The wings of bats and birds are an example of convergent evolution because, despite the fact that the wings of bats and birds have similar structures and functions, bats are mammals and are therefore not closely related to birds. **10.** Does the animal, at some point in its life, have each of the following features: notochord; dorsal, hollow nerve cord; tail that extends beyond the anus; and pharyngeal pouches?

Section Review 33-2

1. The control of body temperature is important for an organism because many life functions are carried out best within a narrow temperature range.
2. a source of heat for the body, a way to conserve heat, and a way to eliminate heat **3.** ectotherm
4. endotherm **5.** endotherm **6.** ectotherm
7. endotherm **8.** endotherm **9.** Possible answers: An alligator is an ectotherm and therefore would bask in the sun when the environmental temperature is cool and move to the shade when the environmental temperature is warm. **10.** Both birds and mammals are endotherms. Birds conserve body heat through the use of insulating feathers. Mammals use body fat and hair as insulation and can get rid of excess heat by panting or sweating.

Section Review 33-3

1. Carnivores have short digestive tracts that produce enzymes that aid in digesting meat. Herbivores have long intestines that contain bacteria that help digest the fibers in plant tissue. **2.** gills and lungs
3. The chambers and partitions of the heart separate oxygen-rich blood from oxygen-poor blood.
4. Aquatic amphibians and most fishes excrete ammonia from gills into the water. In animals with kidneys, nitrogenous wastes are converted into less toxic compounds that are filtered from the blood by the kidneys. **5.** Nonvertebrate chordates have a mass of nerve cells that form a brain. Vertebrates have a brain with distinct regions, each serving a different function. **6.** The skeletal and muscular systems support a vertebrate's body and allow it to control movement. **7.** amphibian **8.** fish
9. mammal

Chapter Vocabulary Review

1. A notochord is a flexible, supporting structure found only in chordates. **2.** Adaptative radiation is a rapid growth in the diversity of a group of organisms as they adapt to new conditions. **3.** An animal whose body temperature is mainly determined by the environment is an ectotherm. **4.** An endotherm is an animal that is able to control its body temperature from within. **5.** An alveolus is a bubblelike structure found in mammalian lungs that provides an enormous surface area for gas exchange. **6.** A single-loop circulatory system is one in which blood travels in one circuit from the heart to the gills, then to the rest of the body, and back to the heart.
7. A double-loop circulatory system is one in which the first loop carries blood between the heart and the lungs and the second loop carries blood between the heart and the body. **8.** ectotherm **9.** endotherm
10. ectotherm **11.** endotherm **12.** ectotherm **13.** d
14. a **15.** a **16.** b **17.** b **18.** c **19.** a **20.** b

Enrichment

1. Dead soft-bodied animals must be protected from scavengers and decomposition in order to eventually become fossilized. **2.** Since the Burgess Shale was formed by deposits of fine clay mud, it is a sedimentary rock.

Graphic Organizer

1. Vertebrae (backbone) **2.** Jaws and paired appendages **3.** Four limbs **4.** Amniotic egg
5. Endothermy

Chapter 33—Test A

Multiple Choice **1.** D **2.** A **3.** D **4.** A **5.** A **6.** A
7. D **8.** B **9.** D **10.** B **11.** A **12.** A **13.** C **14.** B **15.** A
Completion **16.** adaptive radiations **17.** ectotherm
18. filter feeder **19.** alveoli **20.** cerebrum **Short Answer** **21.** The ecological conditions probably were similar. **22.** Animal B is the ectotherm because ectotherms have lower metabolic rates than endotherms. **23.** No, tunicates have survived to the present day, so their organ systems are well equipped to perform the essential functions of life. **24.** The digestive tracts of carnivores produce enzymes that help digest meat, while the digestive tracts of herbivores often have colonies of bacteria that help digest cellulose fibers in plant tissues. **25.** Larval tunicates swim with a fishlike movement of their muscular tails, whereas adult tunicates either swim by using their siphons or remain attached to a surface. **Using Science Skills** **26.** Vessels C and D contain oxygen-rich blood, and vessels A and B contain oxygen-poor blood. **27.** E and H are atria, F and G are ventricles.
28. to capillaries in the lungs and the rest of the body
29. Crocodilians, birds, and mammals have a circulatory system that is represented by diagram I. Non-crocodilian reptiles have a circulatory system that is represented by diagram II. **30.** The heart in diagram I has two separate ventricles, whereas the heart in diagram II has a single, partially divided ventricle. Hence, mixing of oxygen-rich and oxygen-poor blood does not occur in the heart shown in diagram I, but some mixing does occur in diagram II. **Essay** **31.** Many of the chemical reactions that are important in metabolism are affected by temperature. Therefore, essential life functions can be carried out most efficiently when an animal's body temperature is within a particular operating range. **32.** One hypothesis is that dinosaurs were endotherms. A second hypothesis is that endothermy evolved long after the appearance of the dinosaurs. Evidence suggests that endothermy evolved once along the evolutionary line of reptiles that led to birds and once along the evolutionary line of reptiles that led to mammals. **33.** In mammals, inhaling brings

oxygen-rich air into the lungs through the trachea and many small branches, and exhaling forces oxygen-poor air out of the lungs in the reverse direction through the same passageways. In birds, a system of tubes within the lungs and air sacs attached to the lungs ensures that air flows in only one direction through the lungs. Thus, the gas-exchange surfaces are constantly in contact with fresh air, and stale air is never trapped in the lungs. **34.** The hearts of fishes have two chambers: one atrium and one ventricle. The hearts of amphibians and all reptiles except crocodilians have three chambers: two atria and one ventricle. In those reptiles, however, the ventricle contains a partial partition. The hearts of crocodilians, birds, and mammals have four chambers: two atria and two ventricles. **35.** Tunicates, aquatic amphibians, and most fishes excrete ammonia. Mammals, land amphibians, and cartilaginous fishes convert ammonia into urea, which is excreted. Reptiles and birds change ammonia into uric acid.

Chapter 33—Test B

Multiple Choice **1.** C **2.** B **3.** B **4.** B **5.** B **6.** B **7.** B **8.** C **9.** A **10.** C **11.** C **12.** A **13.** B **14.** B **15.** C
Completion **16.** lancelets **17.** ectothermy **18.** alveoli **19.** double **20.** viviparous **Short Answer** **21.** a notochord, a dorsal hollow nerve cord, a tail that extends posterior to the anus, and pharyngeal pouches **22.** a source of heat for the body, a way to conserve that heat, and a method of eliminating excess heat when necessary **23.** One loop carries blood between the heart and the lungs, while the other loop carries blood between the heart and the rest of the body. **24.** Vertebrate kidneys excrete nitrogenous wastes and regulate the amount of water in the body. **25.** The optic lobes are involved in vision, and the olfactory bulbs are involved in the sense of smell.
Using Science Skills **26.** the litopterns **27.** during the Early Cenozoic **28.** Accept any two: mastodons, condylarths, creodonts, litopterns. **29.** proboscideans **30.** chiropterans

Chapter 34 Animal Behavior

Answers for the Adapted Reading and Study Workbook (worksheets pp. 170–176) can be found in the Adapted Reading and Study Workbook, Annotated Teacher's Edition.

Answers for the Reading and Study Workbook (worksheets pp. 179–184) can be found in the Reading and Study Workbook, Annotated Teacher's Edition.

Section 34-1

1. behavior **2.** stimulus **3.** body systems **4.** brain **5.** Innate behavior, also known as instinct, appears in fully functional form the first time it is performed. One example of innate behavior is a spider building a web. **6.** Habituation **7.** An animal makes a mental connection between a stimulus and some kind of reward or punishment. **8.** Operant Conditioning **9.** Possible answer: Monkeys learned to stack boxes on top of one another to reach bananas hanging overhead. **10.** Possible answers include: Take the dog for car rides frequently, so it becomes habituated to the movement of the car. Alternatively, give the dog a treat, such as a dog biscuit, every time it enters the car, so that the dog becomes conditioned to associate entering the car with a pleasant experience.

Section 34-2

1. environment **2.** migration **3.** circadian rhythms **4.** courtship **5.** society **6.** Communication **7.** Aggression is threatening behavior that one animal uses to gain control over another. One example is lions in a pride snapping and snarling at one another as they compete for food. **8.** Evolutionary success is measured by an animal's ability to pass on its set of genes. Helping a relative survive increases the chance that the genes an individual shares with that relative will be passed along to the next generation of offspring. **9.** Possible answer: A city or town is similar to an animal society in that it consists of many individuals who interact with one another, many working together. Unlike animal societies, most people in a city or town are not closely related to one another. In addition, while people in small groups within the community may cooperate, only a few people work together for the benefit of the entire community. **10.** Possible answer: In the summer, when there is more daylight, I'm awake longer. In the winter, when there is less daylight, I wake up later and go to bed earlier.

Chapter Vocabulary Review

1. (across) imprinting **1.** (down) innate **2.** behavior **3.** learning **4.** language **5.** habituation **6.** stimulus **7.** operant **8.** response **9.** migration **10.** rhythm **11.** classical **12.** territory **13.** communication **14.** insight **15.** a **16.** b **17.** c **18.** a **19.** c **20.** d

Enrichment

1. Animals that hibernate seem to have an annual clock that is set to changes in the amount of light and temperature. **2.** Students' charts should include the following: preparation for hibernation (cessation of shivering, reduced blood flow, and suppressed heart rate); hibernation (lowered body temperature and reduced body functions); and waking from hibernation (increased body heat, blood circulation, heart rate, and hunger).

Graphic Organizer

1. Innate behaviors **2.** Learned behaviors (Learning)
3. Operant conditioning **4.** Insight learning
5. Response to a repetitive stimulus

Chapter 34—Test A

Multiple Choice **1.** A **2.** D **3.** C **4.** C **5.** C **6.** B
7. B **8.** C **9.** C **10.** B **11.** A **12.** D **13.** C **14.** B **15.** A
Completion **16.** stimulus **17.** habituation **18.**
threatening (harmful) **19.** classical conditioning
20. communication **Short Answer** **21.** Innate
behaviors help an animal survive. Many innate behaviors, such as a spider's building a web or the suckling of a newborn mammal, help the animal to get food. Others, such as nest building, help an animal to reproduce. **22.** In habituation, an animal decreases or stops its response to a repetitive stimulus that is nonthreatening or unrewarding, which allows the animal to spend its time and energy more efficiently.
23. Young geese have an innate urge to follow the first moving object they see, but they must learn from experience what object to follow. **24.** When food or other resources are scarce, dormancy and migration allow animals to survive by becoming inactive or by moving to another place where resources are more plentiful. **25.** The members of a society usually share a large proportion of one another's genes, so helping other members survive increases the chance that an animal's own genes will be passed to the next generation. **Using Science Skills** **26.** innate **27.** the female **28.** the male, because the male must guide the female to the nest **29.** The male swims zigzag to the female, swims toward the nest, points to the nest, trembles, and nudges the female. **30.** The female gives a head-up display, swims head-up toward the male, enters the nest, lays eggs in the nest, and leaves the nest. **Essay** **31.** Some behaviors can be inherited by an animal's offspring because these behaviors are influenced by genes. Sometimes a new adaptive behavior that is influenced by genes helps an individual to survive and reproduce better than individuals that do not have the behavior. After many generations of natural selection, most individuals in the population will have the new adaptive behavior.
32. In classical conditioning, an animal learns to make a mental connection between a stimulus and some kind of reward or punishment. The stimulus is one that the animal did not previously associate with the reward or punishment. In operant conditioning, an animal learns through trial and error to produce a certain behavior to receive a reward or avoid punishment. **33.** A Skinner box is a box in which an animal is placed to test for the ability to learn by operant conditioning. The box contains a button or lever that, when pressed, delivers a food reward. After the animal is rewarded several times, it learns that it can receive food whenever it presses the button or lever. At that point, the animal has learned by operant conditioning how to obtain food. **34.** Territories contain resources, such as food and water, that enable the animal to survive and reproduce. By claiming a territory, an animal keeps other animals away. **35.** Communication can occur whenever one individual passes information to another. Animals may use visual, sound, touch, or chemical signals to communicate with one another. Animals use these signals to communicate such things as warnings, readiness to mate, and the boundaries of a territory.

Chapter 34—Test B

Multiple Choice **1.** C **2.** C **3.** B **4.** A **5.** A **6.** C
7. A **8.** C **9.** C **10.** A **11.** B **12.** B **13.** C **14.** A
15. C **Completion** **16.** response **17.** Ivan Pavlov
18. insight **19.** aggression **20.** language **Short
Answer** **21.** the sense organs, the nervous system, and the muscles **22.** An innate behavior is a behavior that appears in fully functional form the first time it is performed and does not require previous experience with the stimulus that triggers it. **23.** habituation, classical conditioning, operant conditioning, and insight learning **24.** Courtship helps individuals attract, locate, and mate with other members of the same species and can help animals identify healthy mates. **25.** visual, sound, touch, and chemical signals **Using Science Skills** **26.** innate behavior
27. classical conditioning **28.** Food and a ringing bell are the two stimuli. The response is salivation by the dog. **29.** habituation, operant conditioning, and insight learning **30.** imprinting

Unit 9—Test A

Multiple Choice **1.** C **2.** D **3.** B **4.** A **5.** D **6.** B **7.** B
8. D **9.** C **10.** A **11.** D **12.** A **13.** C **14.** B **15.** D
Completion **16.** amphibian **17.** four-chambered
18. Triassic Period **19.** invertebrate **20.** response; stimulus **Short Answer** **21.** Both tunicates and lancelets have a hollow nerve cord, a notochord, pharyngeal pouches, and a tail at some stage of their life cycle. **22.** Amphibians require water for reproduction and for the development of their fishlike embryos.
23. Some adaptations that enable birds to fly include highly efficient digestive, respiratory, and circulatory systems; aerodynamic feathers and wings; strong, lightweight bones; and strong chest muscles. **24.** Primates have binocular vision, a well-developed cerebrum, relatively long fingers and toes, and arms that can rotate around their shoulder joints. **25.** When an animal's senses have detected an external stimulus, the information is passed along nerve cells to the

brain. The brain and other parts of the nervous system process the information and direct body muscles to produce the response. **Using Science Skills 26.** The cow **27.** The shark is a carnivore. The cow and the pigeon are herbivores. Herbivores have long intestines to help digest plant tissues. Carnivores have short digestive tracts.

28. Because birds and mammals are endotherms, they require large amounts of food to supply the energy for their high metabolic rate. Ectothermic fishes do not require as much energy from food because they have a much lower metabolic rate. **29.** The pigeon has a crop and a gizzard. The crop stores and moistens food before it moves toward the stomach. The gizzard is a muscular part of the stomach that breaks down food by crushing and grinding it. **30.** Cows have flat-edged incisors to grasp and tear plants and broad, flattened molars to grind the food. **Essay 31.** Like in the evolution of other chordate groups, a series of complex adaptive radiations produced a large number of species. These adaptive radiations occurred in response to new environmental conditions or the appearance of new adaptations.

32. Humans are the only animals known to use language. Humans are capable of learning and using language because of their well-developed brain. The cerebrum is greatly enlarged, compared with that of other vertebrates, and includes a well-developed cerebral cortex. **33.** Aquatic vertebrates, such as fishes and larval amphibians, use gills for respiration. Adult amphibians, reptiles, birds, and mammals use lungs to breathe. As you move from amphibians to mammals, lungs become more complex and efficient at obtaining oxygen from air. Reptilian lungs often are divided into chambers that increase the surface area for gas exchange. Mammals have thousands of bubblelike alveoli that produce a very large area for gas exchange. Birds have the most efficient respiratory system. Their system of air sacs and tubes in the lungs enables a one-way air flow. This ensures that the lungs are in constant contact with oxygen-rich air. **34.** The chemical reactions for essential life functions are carried out most efficiently when an animal's internal body temperature is within a certain range. Animals control their body temperature either with their behavior (ectotherms) or by generating their own heat and conserving it with body insulation

(endotherms). **35.** The behavior of an animal determines whether it will get food and other resources, find a mate, and get protection from predators. If an animal has an adaptive behavior that makes it better suited to get any of the things it needs, it will have a better chance of surviving and passing its genes to offspring.

Unit 9—Test B

Multiple Choice 1. C **2.** B **3.** C **4.** B **5.** A **6.** C **7.** A **8.** A **9.** C **10.** B **11.** C **12.** A **13.** A **14.** B **15.** C **Completion 16.** jaws and paired fins **17.** shell **18.** opposable thumb **19.** endotherm **20.** stimulus; response **Short Answer 21.** This chordate, a fish, is adapted to an aquatic lifestyle. It has fins and gills, adaptations for moving and getting oxygen in water. **22.** The embryos of both birds and reptiles develop within amniotic eggs. Both excrete nitrogenous wastes as uric acid and have a cloaca. Both have similar bones that support the front and hind limbs. **23.** Mammalian kidneys filter urea from the blood, as well as excrete excess water or retain needed water. **24.** Adaptive radiations occurred with a rapid increase in the number and diversity of species as they adapted to new conditions. Convergent evolution occurred when unrelated species evolved similar adaptations to similar environments. **25.** Members of a society are often closely related, and therefore, share a large proportion of each other's genes. Helping a relative survive increases the chance that the genes an individual shares with the relative will be passed along to offspring. **Using Science Skills 26.** Diagram III **27.** The circulatory system in diagram III supports gills. The circulatory systems in diagrams I and II support lungs. **28.** The heart in diagram I has four chambers. Oxygen-rich blood and oxygen-poor blood are completely separated by the septum. In diagram II, the heart contains three chambers. The ventricle has a partition. **29.** Three-chambered hearts, such as this one, are found in all reptiles except crocodiles and alligators. **30.** The circulatory system in diagram I is most efficient at delivering oxygen because oxygen-rich blood is always completely separated from oxygen-poor blood.

Means of Support

Imagine that you are on a camping trip. You arrive at your campsite and the first thing you do is put up your tent.

1. What purpose do the tent poles serve?

2. How would moving around and sleeping in the tent be affected if you had forgotten the tent poles at home?

3. What types of animals have a means of support that functions like tent poles? Why would such a means of support be beneficial to these animals?

© Pearson Education, Inc.

ANSWERS
1. Poles provide support and hold up the fabric of the tent to people a space.
2. The fabric of the tent would collapse and hang down onto people in the tent. There wouldn't be an open space in which to move around inside the tent.
3. Vertebrates. A skeleton provides support and creates a space inside for internal organs and the like.

30–1 The Chordates

A. What Is a Chordate?

B. Most Chordates Are Vertebrates

C. Nonvertebrate Chordates

   1. Tunicates

   2. Lancelets

© Pearson Education, Inc.

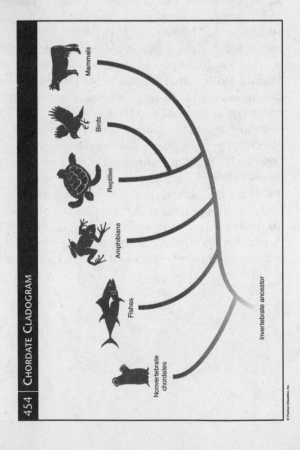

© Pearson Education, Inc.

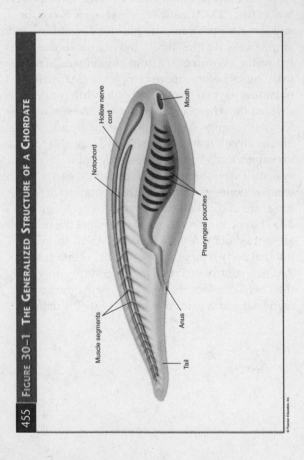

© Pearson Education, Inc.

A Fishy Picture

On a sheet of paper, draw a large diagram of a fish that is familiar to you. Provide as much detail as you can, and label as many parts as possible.

Some of the functions of fishes are as follows: locomotion, respiration, feeding, protection, response, and waste removal. Next to each structure label on your drawing, write the associated function in parentheses. How is each structure related to its function?

30-2 Fishes

A. What Is a Fish?

B. Evolution of Fishes

  1. The First Fishes

  2. The Age of Fishes

  3. The Arrival of Jaws and Paired Fins

  4. The Rise of Modern Fishes

C. Form and Function in Fishes

  1. Feeding

  2. Respiration

  3. Circulation

  4. Excretion

  5. Response

  6. Movement

  7. Reproduction

D. Groups of Fishes

  1. Jawless Fishes

  2. Sharks and Their Relatives

  3. Bony Fishes

E. Ecology of Fishes

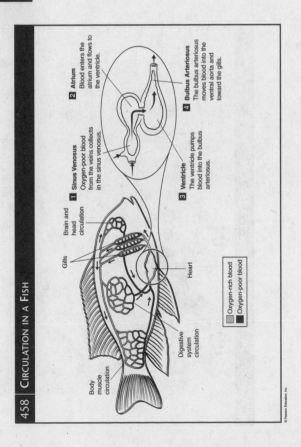

458 | CIRCULATION IN A FISH

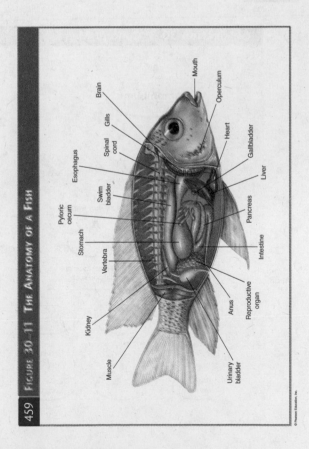

459 | FIGURE 30-11 THE ANATOMY OF A FISH

Declining Numbers of Frogs

Ecologists have recently noticed declining numbers of certain types of amphibians in a variety of places. Some scientists have hypothesized that this decline might be a result of toxins in the environment.

Work with a partner to discuss and answer the questions that follow.

1. What characteristics of amphibians might make them more susceptible to environmental toxins than other types of animals?

2. Frogs reproduce in water. Why might toxins in aquatic ecosystems affect the reproductive success of frogs?

3. Can you think of any other possible explanations for the reduced numbers of amphibians observed?

ANSWERS:
1. Amphibians live both in water and on land, have moist skins that allow the exchange of substances, and do not have protective scales or a thick impermeable skin.
2. Eggs and tadpoles may be more sensitive to toxins in the water during these developmental stages.
3. Possible answers: more predators; presence of a viral, bacterial, or fungal infection; decreasing food supply; and normal fluctuations in population size.

30–3 Amphibians

  A. What Is an Amphibian?

  B. Evolution of Amphibians

  C. Form and Function of Amphibians

    1. Feeding

    2. Respiration

    3. Circulation

    4. Excretion

    5. Reproduction

    6. Movement

    7. Response

  D. Groups of Amphibians

    1. Salamanders

    2. Frogs and Toads

    3. Caecilians

  E. Ecology of Amphibians

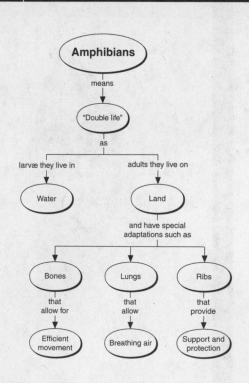

Adults are typically ready to breed in about one to two years.

Adult Frog

Frog eggs are laid in water and undergo external fertilization.

Fertilized Eggs

The eggs hatch into tadpoles a few days to several weeks later.

Tadpoles

Tadpoles gradually grow limbs, lose their tails and gills, and become meat-eaters as they develop into terrestrial adults.

Young Frog

Out on Dry Land

Think about animals that live in the water and the features they share. When animals moved onto dry land, decreased availability of water presented new problems for them. Think about the challenges posed by the "move onto dry land."

With a partner, describe how each of the following characteristics exhibited by reptiles allows for life on land and how these characteristics differ from those of water-dwelling animals.

1. Dry, scaly skin

2. Lungs

3. Shelled eggs

ANSWERS
1. Dry, scaly skin prevents water loss and provides protection. Water-dwelling animals do not have dry skin.
2. Lungs allow reptiles to obtain oxygen from the air; most water-dwelling animals have gills to obtain oxygen from water.
3. Shelled eggs have a protective shell and membrane that prevents the embryo from drying out; most water-dwelling animals do not lay shelled eggs.

31–1 Reptiles

A. What Is a Reptile?

B. Evolution of Reptiles
  1. Mammal-like Reptiles
  2. Enter the Dinosaurs
  3. Exit the Dinosaurs

C. Form and Function in Reptiles
  1. Body Temperature Control
  2. Feeding
  3. Respiration
  4. Circulation
  5. Excretion
  6. Response
  7. Movement
  8. Reproduction

D. Groups of Reptiles
  1. Lizards and Snakes
  2. Crocodilians
  3. Turtles and Tortoises
  4. Tuataras

E. Ecology of Reptiles

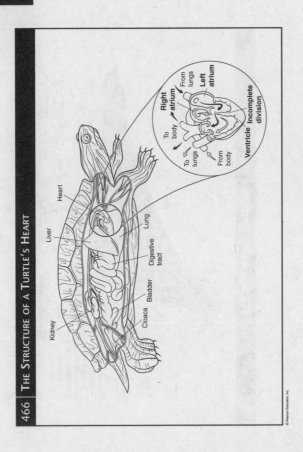

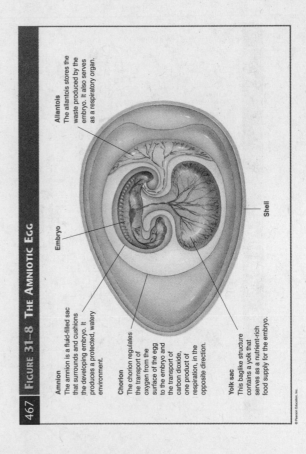

Allantois
The allantois stores the waste produced by the embryo. It also serves as a respiratory organ.

Amnion
The amnion is a fluid-filled sac that surrounds the developing embryo. It produces a protected, watery environment.

Chorion
The chorion regulates the transport of oxygen from the surface of the egg to the embryo and the transport of carbon dioxide, one product of respiration, in the opposite direction.

Yolk sac
This baglike structure contains a yolk that serves as a nutrient-rich food supply for the embryo.

Embryo

Shell

Silent Spring

Rachel Carson wrote the book *Silent Spring* in the 1960s. As the title suggests, she describes waking up on a spring morning, hearing none of the usual chirping of songbirds and wondering what happened to them. Carson's book increased awareness of the use of pesticides in the environment. Unfortunately, one of the chemicals that had been used interfered with the formation of the shells of birds' eggs.

With a partner, discuss and answer the questions that follow.

1. What effect would weak eggshells have on the population of birds ? How might this cause a "silent spring?"

2. If you were a legislator, what would you do about the use of chemicals such as pesticides in our environment?

31–2 Birds

A. What Is a Bird?

B. Evolution of Birds

C. Form, Function, and Flight

   1. Body Temperature Control

   2. Feeding

   3. Respiration

   4. Circulation

   5. Excretion

   6. Response

   7. Movement

   8. Reproduction

D. Groups of Birds

E. Ecology of Birds

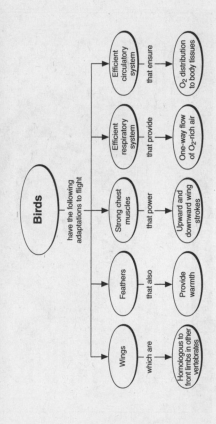

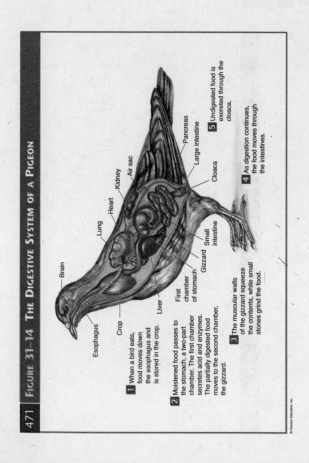

1 When a bird eats, food moves down the esophagus and is stored in the crop.

2 Moistened food passes to the stomach, a two-part chamber. The first chamber secretes acid and enzymes. The partially digested food moves to the second chamber, the gizzard.

3 The muscular walls of the gizzard squeeze the contents, while small stones grind the food.

4 As digestion continues, the food moves through the intestines.

5 Undigested food is excreted through the cloaca.

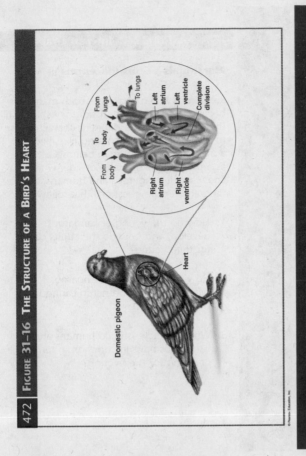

Domestic pigeon

Heart

From lungs
To lungs
Left atrium
Left ventricle
Complete division
To body
From body
Right atrium
Right ventricle

A Warm Body

Because mammals and birds generate heat within their bodies, they are endotherms. Other types of chordates control body temperature by behavior. These animals are ectotherms.

1. Mammals and birds eat much more food than do other types of chordates. Why do you think this is necessary?

2. What body features do endotherms have that would provide insulation to conserve heat produced within the body? Would you expect ectotherms to have such features?

3. What are two examples of endotherms? What is the specific type of insulation that each one has?

32–1 Introduction to the Mammals

A. Evolution of Mammals

B. Form and Function in Mammals

1. Body Temperature Control

2. Feeding

3. Respiration

4. Circulation

5. Excretion

6. Response

7. Chemical Controls

8. Fighting Disease

9. Movement

10. Reproduction

11. Interrelationships of Organ Systems

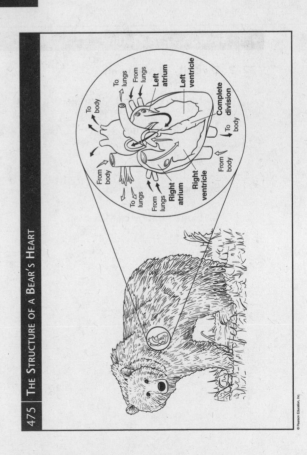

To lungs
From lungs
Left atrium
Left ventricle
Complete division
To body
To body
From body
From body
To lungs
From lungs
Right atrium
Right ventricle

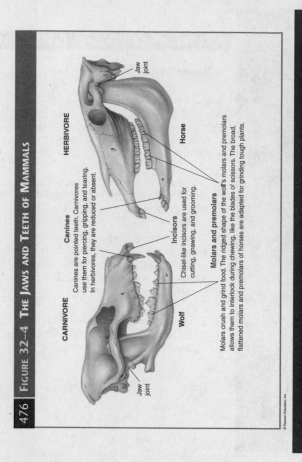

HERBIVORE

Canines
Canines are pointed teeth. Carnivores use them for piercing, gripping, and tearing. In herbivores, they are reduced or absent.

Horse

Incisors
Chisel-like incisors are used for cutting, gnawing, and grooming.

Molars and premolars
Molars crush and grind food. The ridged shape of the wolf's molars and premolars allows them to interlock during chewing, like the blades of scissors. The broad, flattened molars and premolars of horses are adapted for grinding tough plants.

CARNIVORE

Wolf

Jaw joint

© Pearson Education, Inc.

Marsupials Versus Placentals

Kangaroos and humans are both mammals because of the characteristics they share. Still, they display enough different characteristics to result in a kangaroo being classified as a marsupial and a human being classified as a placental mammal. Consider what you know about kangaroos and humans, and then answer the questions that follow.

1. How do the young of kangaroos develop, and how do the adults care for their young?

2. How do humans and kangaroos differ from one another in caring for their young?

3. What characteristic do humans and kangaroos have in common in terms of caring for their young?

ANSWERS
1. Kangaroos bear live, underdeveloped young that complete their development in an external pouch, where they attach to a nipple for nourishment.
2. Human babies require care (feeding, protecting, providing a place to live) for a longer time. Human parents teach their offspring more than any other animals do.
3. Newborns feed on the mother's milk that is produced by mammary glands.

© Pearson Education, Inc.

32–2 Diversity of Mammals

A. Monotremes and Marsupials

   1. Monotremes

   2. Marsupials

B. Placental Mammals

C. Biogeography of Mammals

© Pearson Education, Inc.

Orders of Placental Mammals

Order	Characteristics	Examples
Insectivores	Long, narrow snouts, sharp claws	Shrews, hedgehogs, moles
Sirenians	Water-dwelling, slow-moving	Manatees, dugongs
Cetaceans	Live and breed in ocean, come to surface to breathe	Whales, dolphins
Chiropterans	Winged, capable of true flight	Bats
Rodents	Single pair of long, curved incisor teeth in upper and lower jaws	Mice, rats, voles, squirrels, beavers, porcupines, chinchillas
Perissodactyls	Hoofed, with an odd number of toes on each foot	Horses, tapirs, rhinoceroses, zebras
Carnivores	Sharp teeth and claws	Tigers, hyenas, dogs, foxes, bears, raccoons, walruses
Artiodactyls	Hoofed, with an even number of toes on each foot	Cattle, sheep, goats, pigs, ibex, giraffes, hippopotami, camels
Proboscideans	Trunks	Asian and African elephants, mastodons and mammoths
Lagomorphs	Two pairs of incisors in upper jaw, hind legs allow leaping	Snowshoe hares, rabbits
Xenarthrans	No teeth (or very small teeth in the back of the jaw)	Sloths, anteaters, armadillos
Primates	Highly developed cerebrum and complex behaviors	Lemurs, tarsiers, apes, gibbons, macaques, humans

© Pearson Education, Inc.

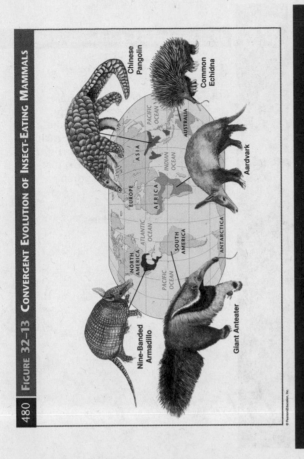

480 | **Figure 32–13** Convergent Evolution of Insect-Eating Mammals

481 | **Section 32–3** Interest Grabber

Skeletal Features of Primates

Recall that primates are an order of mammals. One difference that exists between primates and other mammals is in the structure of the primate skeleton. Some examples of primates include humans, lemurs, monkeys, and apes.

1. How are the external features of your hands different from the external features of the paws of a dog or the hooves of a horse?

2. Primates are bipedal, or capable of walking on two limbs. What is an advantage of being bipedal?

3. What are some characteristics of your skeleton that enable you to stand and walk?

ANSWERS
1. The human hand has fingers and is capable of manipulating objects, which might allow the use of tools.
2. Arms would be available for many uses; might allow a better view of the environment.
3. Answers may include: the curves of the spine, the width of the pelvis, and the length of the leg bones.

482 | **Section 32–3** Outline

32–3 Primates and Human Origins

A. What Is a Primate?
   1. Fingers, Toes, and Shoulders
   2. Well-Developed Cerebrum
   3. Binocular Vision

B. Evolution of Primates
   1. Prosimians
   2. Anthropoids

C. Hominid Evolution
   1. Early Hominids
   2. *Australopithecus*
   3. *Paranthropus*
   4. Recent Hominid Discoveries
   5. Rethinking Early Hominid Evolution

D. The Road to Modern Humans
   1. The Genus *Homo*
   2. Out of Africa—But Who and When?

E. Modern *Homo sapiens*

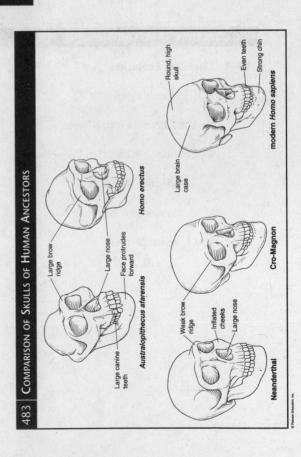

483 | Comparison of Skulls of Human Ancestors

© Pearson Education, Inc., publishing as Pearson Prentice Hall.

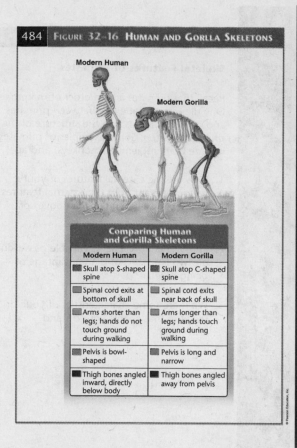

Modern Human

Modern Gorilla

Comparing Human and Gorilla Skeletons

Modern Human	Modern Gorilla
Skull atop S-shaped spine	Skull atop C-shaped spine
Spinal cord exits at bottom of skull	Spinal cord exits near back of skull
Arms shorter than legs; hands do not touch ground during walking	Arms longer than legs; hands touch ground during walking
Pelvis is bowl-shaped	Pelvis is long and narrow
Thigh bones angled inward, directly below body	Thigh bones angled away from pelvis

© Pearson Education, Inc.

Covering the Chordates

Though all chordates share certain characteristics, they are extremely diverse. With a partner, identify the characteristic body covering for each of the six major groups of animals listed below. Then, explain how that covering is useful for that group of animals.

1. Nonvertebrate chordates

2. Fishes

3. Amphibians

4. Reptiles

5. Birds

6. Mammals

ANSWERS
1. Nonvertebrate chordates: tough covering or skin provides protection
2. Fishes: scales (or skin) provides protection; reduces friction
3. Amphibians: thin, moist skin allows exchange of oxygen and carbon dioxide
4. Reptiles: dry, scaly skin prevents drying out; provides protection
5. Birds: feathers provide insulation; enable flight
6. Mammals: fur, skin, hair, etc.; provides insulation and protection

© Pearson Education, Inc.

33–1 Chordate Evolution

A. Chordate Origins

B. The Chordate Family Tree

C. Evolutionary Trends in Vertebrates

  1. Adaptive Radiations

  2. Convergent Evolution

D. Chordate Diversity

© Pearson Education, Inc.

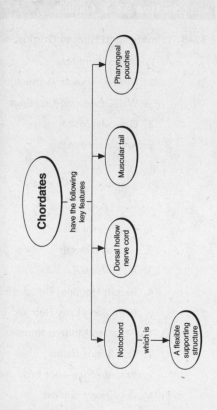

Chordates

have the following key features

Pharyngeal pouches

Muscular tail

Dorsal hollow nerve cord

Notochord — which is — A flexible supporting structure

© Pearson Education, Inc.

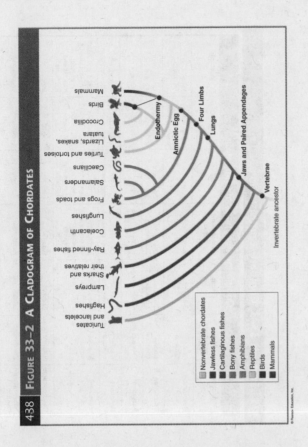

Figure 33–2 A Cladogram of Chordates

© Pearson Education, Inc.

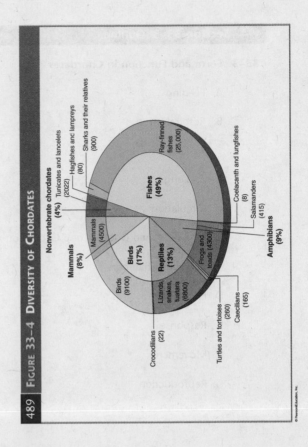

Figure 33–4 Diversity of Chordates

© Pearson Education, Inc.

Section 33–2 Outline

33–2 Controlling Body Temperature

A. Body Temperature and Homeostasis

   1. Ectothermy

   2. Endothermy

B. Comparing Ectotherms and Endotherms

C. Evolution of Temperature Control

© Pearson Education, Inc.

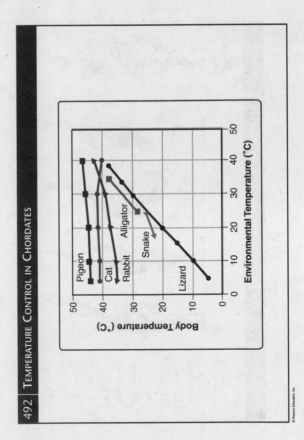

Temperature Control in Chordates

© Pearson Education, Inc.

33–3 Form and Function in Chordates

A. Feeding

B. Respiration

  1. Gills

  2. Lungs

C. Circulation

  1. Single- and Double-Loop Circulation

  2. Heart Chambers

D. Excretion

E. Response

F. Movement

G. Reproduction

© Pearson Education, Inc.

Comparing Functions of Chordates

Function	Non-vertebrate Chordates	Fishes	Amphibians (adult)	Reptiles	Birds	Mammals
Respiration	Gills and diffusion	Gills/air sacs	Simple lungs and skin	Lungs	Lungs (tubes and air sacs; one-way flow)	Lungs (alveoli)
Circulation	No true chambers	Single loop; 2 chambers	Double loop; 3 chambers	Double loop; 3 chambers	Double loop; 4 chambers	Double loop; 4 chambers
Excretion	Gills and gill slits	Kidney and gills	Kidney and gills	Kidney	Kidney	Kidney
Response	Simple; mass of nerve cells	Cephalization; small cerebrum	Cephalization; small cerebrum	Cephalization; small cerebrum	Cephalization; large cerebrum	Cephalization; large cerebrum
Movement	Muscles, no bones	Muscles on either side of backbone	Limbs stick out sideways; muscles and ligaments	Limbs point directly toward ground; muscles and ligaments	Upper limbs are wings; 2 feet; muscles and ligaments	2 or 4 legs; walk with legs straight under them; muscles and ligaments
Reproduction	External fertilization	External fertilization	External fertilization	Internal fertilization; shelled egg	Internal fertilization; shelled egg	Internal fertilization and development
Temperature Control	Ectothermic	Ectothermic	Ectothermic	Ectothermic	Endothermic	Endothermic

© Pearson Education, Inc.

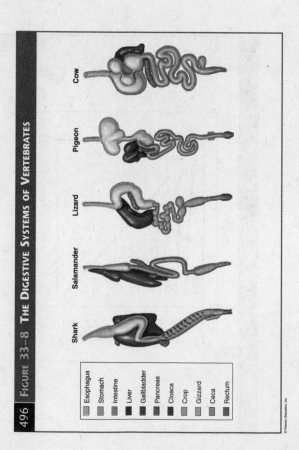

Cow, Pigeon, Lizard, Salamander, Shark

- Esophagus
- Stomach
- Intestine
- Liver
- Gallbladder
- Pancreas
- Cloaca
- Crop
- Gizzard
- Ceca
- Rectum

© Pearson Education, Inc.

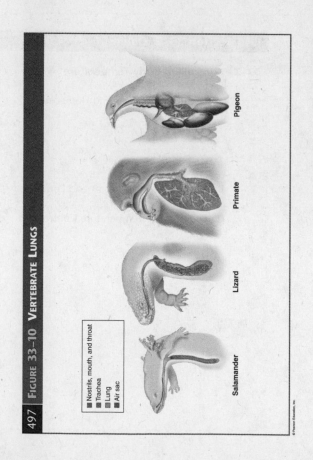

- Nostrils, mouth, and throat
- Trachea
- Lung
- Air sac

Salamander, Lizard, Primate, Pigeon

© Pearson Education, Inc.

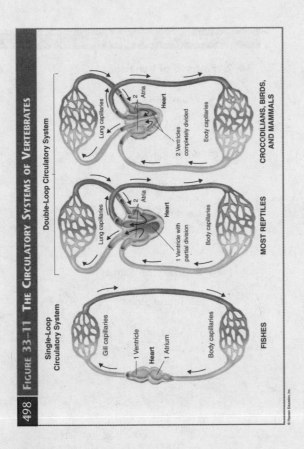

| FIGURE 33–11 THE CIRCULATORY SYSTEMS OF VERTEBRATES

Double-Loop Circulatory System

Lung capillaries
Atria
Heart
2 Ventricles completely divided
Body capillaries

CROCODILIANS, BIRDS, AND MAMMALS

Lung capillaries
Atria
Heart
1 Ventricle with partial division
Body capillaries

MOST REPTILES

Single-Loop Circulatory System

Gill capillaries
1 Ventricle
Heart
1 Atrium
Body capillaries

FISHES

© Pearson Education, Inc.

© Pearson Education, Inc.

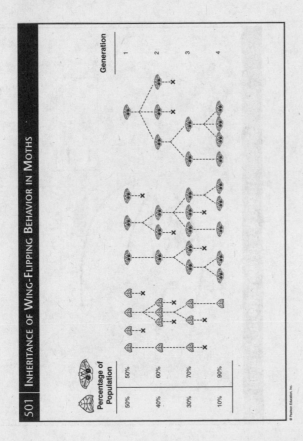

501 | INHERITANCE OF WING-FLIPPING BEHAVIOR IN MOTHS

Generation
1
2
3
4

Percentage of Population

50% | 50%
60% | 40%
70% | 30%
90% | 10%

© Pearson Education, Inc.

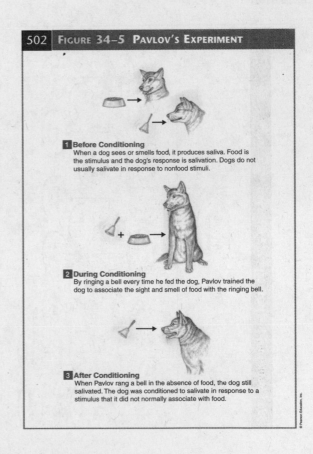

502 | FIGURE 34–5 PAVLOV'S EXPERIMENT

1 Before Conditioning
When a dog sees or smells food, it produces saliva. Food is the stimulus and the dog's response is salivation. Dogs do not usually salivate in response to nonfood stimuli.

2 During Conditioning
By ringing a bell every time he fed the dog, Pavlov trained the dog to associate the sight and smell of food with the ringing bell.

3 After Conditioning
When Pavlov rang a bell in the absence of food, the dog still salivated. The dog was conditioned to salivate in response to a stimulus that it did not normally associate with food.

© Pearson Education, Inc.

How Do You Behave?

In an average day, you exhibit numerous behaviors. Some behaviors are learned and some are innate.

1. Think of a behavior that you can picture yourself doing. What behavior did you choose?

2. When do you think you first exhibited this behavior?

3. What process was involved in the development of this behavior?

4. Do you think this behavior is innate or learned? Explain your answer.

ANSWERS
Students' answers will depend on the type of behavior chosen.
Make sure that students understand the difference between innate
and learned behaviors, as well as the types of learned behavior.

© Pearson Education, Inc.

34–2 Patterns of Behavior

  A. Behavioral Cycles

  B. Courtship

  C. Social Behavior

  D. Competition and Aggression

  E. Communication

    1. Visual Signals

    2. Chemical Signals

    3. Sound Signals

    4. Language

© Pearson Education, Inc.

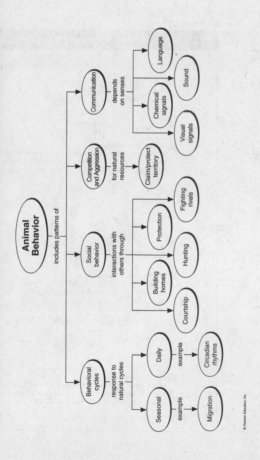

© Pearson Education, Inc.

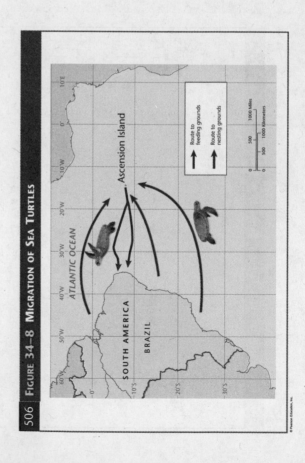

© Pearson Education, Inc.